Feminine Faces

Feminine Faces:

Portraits of Biblical Women of Faith

Randy L. Hyde

Parson's Porch Books
121 Holly Trail Road, NW
Cleveland, Tennessee 37311

Feminine Faces: Portraits of Biblical Women of Faith

Published 2010.
Printed in the United States of America.
ISBN 978-0982-9413-6-2

To order additional copies of this book, contact:

Parson's Porch Books
1-423-475-7308
www.parsonsporch.com

Cover design: Eric Killinger, *Ars Intermundia Expressus*

Dedicated to

Janet

whose feminine face has graced my life

for thirty-six years

TABLE OF CONTENTS

FOREWORD

Only in the last few decades have the stories of biblical women begun to move into the spotlight in biblical interpretation. The reason for the earlier neglect, no doubt, was the perception that the real action in the biblical narratives was between selected men and God. Women were not considered "great heroes" of the faith, even though they always put in appearances in the stories (and do show up in the great roll call of saints in Hebrews 11). The women were considered ancillary to the main story, decorative and distracting. Of course, they *were* necessary to conceive children, but in traditional recounting they occupied the "shadow side" of history. Rarely were they treated as real women with significant stories of their own.

Randy Hyde, pastor of Pulaski Heights Baptist Church in Little Rock, Arkansas, adds a fresh voice to the retrieving of these stories. Our foremothers in faith come alive through his perceptive and imaginative re-telling of the contours of their lives. Attentive to the patriarchal context as well as some of the textual ambiguities in Hebrew and Greek manuscripts, Dr. Hyde renders lively characters through his narrative interpretation. You may feel that you are meeting Sarah; Rebekah; Miriam; Hannah; Mary, the mother of Jesus; Martha; and Mary Magdalene—some of my favorites—for the first time.

Pastoral wisdom shines through his writing. Missing is any sort of glibness that often infects writers struggling with perplexing texts. The ways of God are not readily discernible in many of these vignettes; Dr. Hyde has witnessed enough of the tragic and inexplicable in his many years as a pastor. He knows that God often seems silent, even to the faithful. Thus, he wisely allows the tensions and the meandering plots to demonstrate the partial understanding humans have of divine providence in all its splendid and searing mystery. Dr. Hyde does, however, encourage readers "to remain open to hearing a word from God that comes in a form we have not known before" (64).

Most winsome in his writing is his capacity to see events from the woman's point of view. Whether it is Sarah's bitter laughter over being told she will yet have a child, or Ruth's brave ingenuity in providing for her family and her good faith in the process, or Mary Magdalene's transformation through being called and known in a new way. Not all interpreters will approach these profiles in the same way; however, Dr. Hyde mines rich biblical veins that produce treasure for the contemporary learner. I commend this book to preachers and Bible study groups, as well as individual readers seeking inspiration and guidance.

Molly T. Marshall
Professor of Theology and Spiritual Formation,
Acting Academic Dean
Central Baptist Theological Seminary
Kansas City, Kansas
Ordinary Time, 2004

PREFACE

As I PUT THE FINAL touches to this manuscript, my wife Janet and I are on sabbatical in Scotland. More specifically, we are on the Isle of Iona where, in the sixth century, an Irish missionary named Columba first presented Christianity to the local Picts and Scots. The weather is typically Scottish, even for July: cool, windy, and often rainy. It changes several times during the day, and has spawned a local saying: "Some people walk in the rain... others just get wet." Despite the fickle nature of the weather, there is a serenity to be found here as perhaps in no other place I've ever been, a calm that is conducive to thinking biblically and spiritually.

This book, whose title is borrowed from an old volume of sermons by Clovis Chappell,* is my attempt to put a face on the faithful and brave women of the Bible; women who often lived under difficult circumstances, yet in their own individual ways, sought to do the will of God as they experienced it.

Ironically, St. Columba rid this tiny island of women, and as I look out over the Sound that separates Iona from Mull, I can see the now uninhabited Isle of Women to which they were transported. Evidently, Columba found them to be a "distraction" to his serious work of evangelizing this part of the world. It would be interesting to know what his response

*Clovis Chappell, *Feminine Faces* (New York & Nashville: Abingdon–Cokesbury Press, 1942).

would be to the fact that the good work of worship and service on Iona today is led and promoted by women who mirror the faithfulness of those you will encounter on the following pages.

If this book helps you to a better understanding or deepening of your faith, my effort will have been worth it. But the credit belongs to the faithfulness revealed in the feminine faces of scripture, and the God in whom there is ultimately no "male or female," for we all indeed are one in Christ Jesus.

Randy L. Hyde
Isle of Iona, Scotland
July, 2003

ACKNOWLEDGMENTS

I am indebted to a number of folk who are supporting me in this effort:

My gratitude is expressed to Molly Marshall, a great theologian and good friend, for writing the foreword . . .

My congregation, which granted me a summer away so I could be refreshed and renewed from the rigors of daily pastoral life, not to mention the opportunity to finish this book . . .

My family, who have always encouraged me in my calling and desire to write . . .

The Lilly Foundation that provided me a grant, and therefore made it possible to come to Scotland and find the perfect place to finish this project.

OLD TESTAMENT

EVE

"The Mother of Us All"

So when the woman saw that the tree was good for food, and that it was a delight to the eyes, and that the tree was to be desired to make one wise, she took of its fruit and ate (Genesis 3:6).

This is all it took . . . one little red apple. At least that's generally the way we think about it. Eve took a bite, enticed Adam to do likewise, and the world has never been the same.

Do you remember the cartoons that asked, "What's wrong with this picture?" Well, there are at least two things that are wrong with this picture. One is, of course, that is wasn't necessarily an apple into which Adam and Eve chomped their pearly whites. The writer of Genesis only tells us it was forbidden fruit. It could have been a kumquat, for all we know. The other thing wrong with the picture is a bit more important and has to do with Eve's response to the wily serpent. We generally believe she succumbed to the serpent's temptation when she picked the fruit and took the first bite. But not so. Eve's demise began when she first started giving credence to the serpent's enticing message. Her big mistake was listening to him in the first place. Taking the fruit merely consummated her alienation from God, an alienation which had already begun during her very first conversation with the snake.

Jesus reminds us, in the Sermon on the Mount, that sin is first committed in our thoughts. Later, as recorded in the Gospel of John, he told his disciples it is what comes out of a person that defiles, not what that person takes in. Eve is a perfect illustration of what he means. Her sin didn't begin with the fruit; it began with her desire.

The writer of Genesis tells us the serpent was more crafty than any of the other wild creatures God had made. There's an interesting play on words in the Hebrew language that we don't see in our English translation. The word which tells us the serpent was "more crafty" than the other creatures has the same root as the word for "naked." The woman—and the man—were exposed (if you will excuse the pun) to the shrewd and crafty elements of the world introduced to them by the serpent.

Have you ever wondered why the serpent approached the woman? Perhaps it is because when God told the human creation they were not to partake of the fruit of the tree in the middle of the garden, nor even to touch it, God first gave this prohibition to the man. The woman had not yet been created. That means that she received the information second-hand. Perhaps the serpent surmised, then, that she would be an easier first target.

It all began with a casual conversation. Perhaps they were talking about the weather.

"Sure is nice today, isn't it?"

"Oh yeah. Seventy-two degrees and twenty-eight percent humidity. It just doesn't get any better than this."

"Yeah, they don't call it 'Paradise' for nothing."

"So, what have you and ol' Adam been up to lately?"

"Oh, not much. We named a few more of the animals yesterday, played some chess with the chimpanzees. You know that big, bulky creature with the horn between his eyes? Adam wants to call him a 'rhinoceros.' Can you believe that? I told him it sounded awfully funny, and besides, it's as hard to spell as it is to pronounce. He said I could call it a 'rhino' for short, if that's the way I felt about it. I tell you, that man of mine has some pretty strange ideas. But, I must admit he treats me well. Besides, there's nothing I can do about it anyway. After all, it's not as if there are other fish in the sea. That's another thing . . . 'fish.' 'Fish.' Where in the world did he come up with the word 'fish'?"

"Yeah, that Adam's a real hoot. The food's pretty good too, I hear."

"Oh yes. And everything we see is just ours for the taking. I'm telling you, this is a great world God has created for us. Adam and I are really very happy."

"Wait a minute. Did I hear you correctly? Did you say you can eat *everything*?"

"Uh huh. Well, everything, that is, except the fruit on the big tree in the middle of the garden. God told Adam, and Adam told me, that we not only can't eat the fruit from that tree, but we can't even touch the tree."

"Now let me get this straight. God said you weren't to eat from this tree? God *really* said that? Why?"

"Well, according to Adam, God didn't really say why. God just said that if we touched the tree or ate of its fruit we would die."

"And you believe this?"

"Of course I believe it. Adam hasn't lied to me yet."

"I don't mean Adam, I mean God. You won't die. Do

you know why God told you not to get close to that tree? God knows that if you eat of the fruit you will be like God. And let me tell you, God's not in the God business for the thrill of competition. God has a monopoly, and that's just the way God wants it, believe you me. Why, God is Ma Bell, cable TV, the gas and electric companies all rolled into one. God knows if you eat of that tree you will be able to tell what is good and what is evil, and that's the kind of knowledge the Almighty wants to keep all to himself. God said you would die. Ooh, that's funny. I hadn't heard that one before. That's a good one. 'You will die.' I haven't had a good laugh for a long time. That's rich, that's really rich."

"You mean we won't die if we eat from the tree?"

"Would I lie to you? Go ahead, honey, take a look at the tree; take a good, long look. The food is good. No, the food is great. Compared to this tree, all the other fruit in the garden is chopped liver. And it's nice to look at too, isn't it? Eating some of this fruit will make you wise, sweetie. Go ahead. You won't die. Trust me. Trust me."

And the rest, as they say, is history. A whole lot of history. In fact, it's all the history there is to tell.

It's almost as if the writer of Genesis looks around at the world in which he lives and sees what God's human creation has become. He filters and sifts all this through his faith experience and says with great understatement, "Something has gone wrong, terribly wrong.

We are not what God intended us to be." And he sets out to tell the story that informs us of what God's good world has become in the hands of God's sinful human creation.

Through the years this story has made for some pretty awful theology. For example, it has led for centuries to religious discrimination against women. After all, Eve is the fallen woman, Eve is the temptress of Adam. It all began with Eve. When it comes to sin, Eve is the mother of us all.

Unfortunately, Southern Baptists have fallen prey to this idea. It was June 13, 1984, during the annual meeting of the Southern Baptist Convention. Meeting in Kansas City, it came time for the more than 17,000 messengers to consider the resolutions. The past five years had been the most controversial ever seen in Southern Baptist life. Much of the divisiveness had come from the resolutions passed at the annual meetings, resolutions which carry no real weight but are very powerful tools of influence nonetheless. 1984 would be no different.

The trouble escalated when a resolution surfaced entitled, "On Ordination and the Role of Women in Ministry." It was the final "WHEREAS" that did most of the damage:

> WHEREAS, While Paul commends women and men alike in other roles of ministry and service (Titus 2:1-10), he excludes women from pastoral leadership (1 Tim. 2:12) to preserve a submission God requires because the man was first in creation and the woman was first in the Edenic fall (1 Tim. 2:13ff.).

"[B]ecause the man was first in creation *and the woman was first in the Edenic fall*" (my italics). Just in case you missed the significance of that statement, or you are not sure just exactly what it means, this is an interpretation of what has become a classic theological blunder. According to this resolution, which passed by a 58 to 42 percent vote, women are to be submissive to men because, in the fall to temptation recorded in the Book of Genesis, Eve took the first bite.

Poor Eve. We're now in the twenty-first century and she's still the scapegoat for what ails us.

By the way, when the serpent told Eve, "You will not die," the word for *you* is plural. He's talking about both the woman and the man. Why? Because he knows that if he can get Eve, he'll get Adam too. The man was just as culpable, just as much to blame, as the woman. He makes no protest, does not resist at all when the woman offers it to him. He asks no questions. He simply and silently eats. The woman is not a temptress; they both give in to their mistrust of God's counsel. Just as they are "one flesh" physically and emotionally, so are they "one flesh" in their sin. And now they must operate out of their own resources. They are no longer completely dependent on God for all their needs.

Did you notice in the Genesis account that while the woman plays the lead role in the transgression, it is the man who responds to God's questioning? Perhaps the writer of Genesis is seeking to provide a balance in the story. Both the woman and the man were at fault. Besides, if it is true that man can blame the fall on woman, then why does Paul characterize Adam as the first one to fall? This is obviously more of a complex issue than some would have us believe.

Another thing . . . It is later in Genesis that Adam is given the responsibility of naming his human companion. The name he chooses is "Eve," which means *life*. Not death, not sin, not mess-up, not temptress . . . *life*. Indeed, Eve is the mother of us all, for she is the mother of life, life being the knowledge of good and evil.

The serpent's temptation to the woman is not for her to be evil, but to have *the knowledge* of good and evil. When we choose to go beyond the knowledge of sin and actually become involved in it, we've got no one else to blame but ourselves. At first, Adam and Eve had no such knowledge. Consequently, they had no moral responsibility. There was no need for them to have any kind of ethical behavior. Ethics calls for decision-making and right choices. The knowledge of good and evil provides opportunities as well as temptations. There was none of that before.

It is no accident that Adam and Eve succumbed together to the serpent's tempting message. Sin always involves other persons, and in that sense Eve shows us our humanness. She wanted to be like a god. Don't we all? To know more about life than we know so far, to know more than we have been given to know. Knowledge is power and the thirst for power leads to an even greater thirst. The sin is spiritual pride and the means of procuring it is disobedience. Eve is indeed the mother of us all.

Until her conversation with the serpent, life for Eve was simply of matter of "do this, do that, don't do this, don't do that." Whatever God told her and Adam to do or not do; it was as simple as that. But with the tempting voice of the serpent came new possibilities. The serpent points out that God's good creation presents options in her understanding and behavior, options she has never thought of before. Such options lead to choices, some or many of which are very seductive. When the serpent asks the question and Eve must respond, it can't be a simple yes or no. She has to explain. If they eat of the fruit of the tree of good and knowledge, they will die.

There are times in a court case when a lawyer will ask a question of a witness. Generally, if the witness is considered to be hostile, the lawyer will say, "Just answer the question 'yes' or 'no'." The opposite is true of the conversation between the woman and the serpent. The serpent asks the question in a way that Eve must elaborate. "We may eat of the fruit of the trees in the garden; but God said, 'You shall not eat of the fruit of the tree that is in the middle of the garden, nor shall you touch it, or you shall die.'"

We have something of a problem here, folks, and if we are going to be honest with this biblical story, we must deal with it. It appears the serpent was right. Adam and Eve did not die. But something did die that day: innocence, trust, dependence. The death of innocence gave birth to sin, to blaming, to scapegoating, to the possibilities of evil.

The man Adam says to God. "It wasn't me! It wasn't me! The woman whom you gave to be with me, she gave me fruit from the tree and I ate." Truth be told, he's not really blaming Eve for this transgression; he's blaming God! God created this beguiling creature to be his companion. This is all God's fault! Eve is just a scapegoat.

"It is not my fault." The man points his finger at the woman and the woman blames the serpent. But when God confronts the serpent for his duplicity, the serpent has nothing to say in return. It's ironic, isn't it? The serpent, who started all these problems, is the only one who doesn't blame somebody else. It could be said that he didn't have anyone to blame, but when desperate enough, we can build a straw man, if necessary, an imaginary enemy upon which to cast the blame of our own mistakes. After all, politicians do it all the time. The serpent surely had the opportunity. But maybe, just maybe, he doesn't blame anyone else because he knows he's right. "You will not die; for God knows . . . your eyes will be opened, and you will be like God." The serpent was right.

So, the question this story engenders is, can God be trusted? The serpent didn't think so, and he convinced Eve, and then Adam, to join his side. The basic issue really isn't the knowledge of good and evil; it's trust. Can Adam and Eve trust God to have their best interest at heart?

Think about it. Is that not the root of all our sin? We seek our own best interest, not just because we are so terribly selfish or self-centered, but because we aren't absolutely certain that God will do it for us. We are like a woman who buys herself a birthday present because she's not sure her husband will remember to do it. There may be good reason to justify this kind of behavior.

Just after midnight on June 1, 1999 an American Airlines jet was landing at the Little Rock, Arkansas airport in a terrible lightning storm. The plane crashed after setting down and was split in two. A vocal group from Ouachita Baptist University, my alma mater, was aboard, coming home after an overseas tour. Miraculously, many of the passengers survived, but several did not. One, a fourteen-year-old girl and the daughter of a friend of mine who was director of the Ouachita Singers, died several days later as a result of her injuries. One of the students, who repeatedly returned to the plane to evacuate passengers, and who was from my hometown, died as a result of smoke inhalation.

Let's ask the hard question. Did God have their best interest at heart? Every generation—every generation—has stories like these. I'm sure you do too. Where is God in all of this?

Well, let's go back to our temptation story. Maybe we can find an answer there. Notice that God does not leave the man and woman, nor does the Lord choose to walk elsewhere. The writer of Genesis makes it sound like God is just taking a casual late afternoon stroll when the breezes are good and the temperature is just right. When God

discovers the man and woman to be covered from their nakedness, it is obvious that something is amiss. Remember the play on words. They are now as crafty, as naked, as the serpent. God confronts, not only Adam and Eve, but the serpent as well. God challenges and disciplines them, but the Lord remains loyal to the human creation. God could have said, "Oh my, there goes the neighborhood. I think I'll move out to the suburbs." But God stays with them despite their sin. And God does the same for you and for me.

We can't know why God allows bad things to happen to people, good people or bad. All we can do is see what lies before us at the present moment. God has an eternal view. Only God knows how all of this will turn out in the end. The important thing is that the Lord does not withdraw fellowship from us.

The good news is that this story doesn't end with Eve and the forbidden fruit. After all, we don't call it Genesis for nothing. It is but the beginning of the human story. Eve shows us how to hide from God. Jesus shows us how to come to God. Eve may be the mother of us all, but Jesus has given his life for us all. So the next time you are tempted not to trust God, to think it is better to take matters into your own hands, don't let the snake tell you what to do.

SARAH

"LAUGHTER"

So Sarah laughed to herself, saying, "After I have grown old, and my husband is old, shall I have pleasure" (Genesis 18:12)?

In the previous chapter we asked the question, can God be trusted? This time let's raise the issue of fairness. It is clear from the outset of scripture, and is underlined, punctuated, and sometimes stated boldly, that God does not relate to the human creation on the basis of fairness. Sarah, the wife of Abraham, is a perfect illustration of that. After all, how would you like it if you were chosen as a major player in God's great plan for the world, and God doesn't bother to let you in on it? That's exactly what happened to Sarah.

Let's set the stage . . .

When his name is still Abram, the Lord appears to him and gives him the promise that he will be rewarded greatly and will be the father of God's chosen people. How can that be, Abram asks, since he has no children? Why, his closest heir is a slave. But the Lord insists the promise will be fulfilled. God has Abram look at the skies. "Go ahead," the Lord says to Abram, "count the stars. Not easy, is it? Well, you will have that many descendants and more. Stroll down to the beach. See the sand? Your children will outnumber the granules of sand. Your seed, my good friend Abram, will produce children upon children."

And Abram, good and faithful man that he is, without question believes what his God tells him. And the Lord nods his head and thinks highly of Abram for such simple, yet profound, faith. "The Lord reckoned it to him as righteousness," is the way the Bible says it. That's simply a biblical way of saying that God is pleased with Abram's response.

Evidently, when your name is Abram and you are dealing with God, you must have patience. Lots and lots of patience. Abram was seventy-five years old when God first called him to leave the land of his fathers. He is now ninety-nine and the last twenty-four years have found him gaining a great deal of wealth, just as God has promised. He is truly, truly blessed. But, he is also still wandering around in a tent trying to find a place to call his own, and he is still without a son to carry on his legacy.

The Lord comes to him again. The Lord renews his promise to him. To prove his word, God changes his name from Abram to Abraham, which means "father of many." He talks a lot about Abraham's offspring, and all the time God is talking they both know that Abraham still has no children. Abraham has no children because his wife Sarah is barren.

Let's review. God tells Abraham his descendants will outnumber the stars. Abraham, at the time, has no children. Abraham is ninety-nine years old and his wife, Sarah, is ninety. Even for early biblical times, that is not a successful formula for growing a big family. Whoever heard of a baby being born in the geriatric wing with Medicare picking up the tab? They won't need a midwife; they'll need Merlin the Magician!

This whole thing would be even more humorous if it weren't for the fact that Sarah doesn't even have a say in it. Not one word. It's not as if Sarah isn't aware of God's promise. But knowing something of the science of human reproduction, she doesn't like her chances of being the mother of all these promised children. So, in an act of desperation and perhaps of great faith, she arranges for her servant Hagar to produce a male child for Abraham.

But this isn't what God has in mind, Sarah. Don't do this, Sarah. You'll regret it, Sarah. Wait on God, Sarah.

But Sarah doesn't wait. And, this whole arrangement turns out to be a development that causes Sarah a great deal of anguish. It seemed to be such a good idea when she thought of it, but it really backfires on her. God wants Sarah to be the mother of Abraham's descendants, not Hagar.

Be patient, Sarah, be patient.

Be patient?! How much more patient can she be? She's ninety years old, for crying out loud!! Sarah is so old she doesn't even buy green bananas! It's not that Sarah isn't patient, she's just being realistic. Besides, there is no indication in scripture that God ever revealed the details of his plan to Sarah. God has a close, intimate speaking relationship with Abraham, it seems, but if Sarah was told anything it was always secondhand. And if Abraham ever told Sarah what was on God's mind, we don't know that either; it isn't in the biblical record. Sarah, bless her heart, is left in the dark.

She has absolutely no control over her life and getting Hagar involved in God's promise is a way—a misguided way, but still a way—for her to rise up before God and her husband and say, "I've had enough! I've heard the promises (secondhand, I might add), but I've experienced only emptiness. Let's get this show on the road." The problem is, it's the wrong show and the wrong road.

And then come the three messengers of God. We don't know what it was about them that so quickly clued Abraham in to the fact that they represented a visitation from God, but they were the Hebrew equivalent of New Testament angels and Abraham identifies them immediately. In good near-eastern tradition, he treats them with generous hospitality. He runs into the tent and instructs Sarah to make bread. He has a servant prepare the entree. He stands by while they eat so if they have need of anything he can get it quickly. He is the consummate host.

"Where is your wife Sarah?" they ask. Ah, finally they get around to considering Sarah. And we're thinking it's about time, aren't we? The answer is obvious. Sarah is in the tent where she's supposed to be, the tent being the equivalent of the kitchen. She's also eavesdropping on their conversation. They may be keeping her out of their deliberations, but she has her own way of getting information, doesn't she? One of the messengers says, again to Abraham and not Sarah, "We'll be back, oh, in about nine months. See you in the delivery room when Sarah has your son."

And that's when she laughed.

The writer of Genesis says she laughed to herself, but she probably laughed loud enough so she could hear herself—

after all, she is ninety years old—and that is loud enough for the messengers to hear. One of them says, "Why did Sarah laugh? We're not talking about physical pleasure here, we're talking about getting the job done. God has a plan and she's right in the middle of it. This is not a laughing matter."

And then he says the magic words . . . *Is anything too wonderful for the Lord*?

"See you in nine months." And as they are walking away Sarah sticks her head out of the tent and calls to them—out of fear, we are told—"I didn't laugh." And because God always gets in the last word, the messenger says over his shoulder as he departs, "Oh yes, you did laugh. I heard you. Indeed, Sarah, you laughed. Don't deny it. You laughed."

And she knows he's right. She's been caught in the act. Sarah did indeed laugh. She knew it and she knew they knew it. And they knew she knew they knew it. But sometimes you commit a little white lie because you are afraid. And I can't think of anything that would put more fear into the heart of a ninety-year old woman than to think that she would be giving birth, can you? Yes, indeed, Sarah laughed. Sometimes you laugh because it hurts too much to cry.

Why did it hurt so much? Well, think of the years of barrenness. Think of the many prayers, the desperate prayers, that Sarah has lifted up to the heavens as she asked for her very own child. Think of the silence of God. Nothing is said to Sarah and nothing is done for Sarah. It is quite possible that the years of emptiness have led to bitterness in Sarah's heart.

The bitterness may not be deep, but it is real and it is always there. It is quite possible that her laughter comes from an old, old wound of despair being opened up fresh once again. Sometimes you laugh because it hurts too much to cry.

Sarah is an age-old (forgive another pun!) symbol of a reality that still exists today. She continues to stand for those, especially women, who are powerless in their lives. Sarah, because of the culture in which she lived, had no choices. Her only means of survival was placing her faith in her husband Abraham, who, in his humanness, subjected her more than once to acts of humiliation and shame. And, as we have said, even when God had a special plan for her life, she only heard about it secondhand.

There are many women today, too many women, who function the same way. Their ability to exist is dependent upon the level at which they have invested their emotions in the life and goodwill—or lack of goodwill—in their husband or "significant other." And they are betrayed . . . betrayed by physical violence, by alcoholism, by enforced divorce.[1] When you read of domestic violence perpetrated against a child, how often is such abuse committed by the mother's boyfriend? She allows this evil to exist in her home because she has such a low self-image, and she will allow her boyfriend to do just about anything to her child because she doesn't want to lose him!

We can cluck our tongues and point our fingers, but the reality is, she doesn't know any better and often doesn't have the mental, emotional, spiritual, or financial resources to behave in any other way. It is a steady, and seemingly endless, cycle of violence and abuse, and it is going on in our neighborhoods right now, all the time. And the only thing that can make a real difference is the intervention of God. Sarah exists

1. Mary Zimmer, *Sister Images* (Nashville: Abingdon Press, 1993), p. 110.

today in the lives of those who are powerless to move beyond where they are emotionally, spiritually, and more often than not, physically.

The message of our scriptures and our faith is that "God makes the promised future possible."[2] And while it may appear to be idealistic, God intervenes in situations in which it seems the way is entirely blocked off. God shapes possibilities when everything seems impossible. "The active engagement of God in the midst of the problems of daily life opens up the future rather than closing it down."[3]

So the most crucial statement in this story, and the most important thing ever said to Sarah in her entire life, was not even said to her directly. It was spoken to her husband Abraham. But she heard. Believe me, she heard. *Is anything too wonderful for the Lord*?

A few years ago Sophie Rhys-Jones was in the news for marrying Prince Edward of England. That was news enough, especially in Great Britain. But what really got the public's attention was her request to the Anglican minister conducting the service that he include in her vows the ancient statement that she would love, honor, and obey her husband. A local talk-radio host decided to give some attention to this and fielded phone calls from two ministers: one a Baptist, the other from the Assembly of God. They both explained in a balanced and well-thought-out fashion that this is not the prevailing attitude today . . . that marriage is seen as a partnership in which both persons are equally submissive to one another, and both are to honor and cherish and respect the other. The radio personality's response, of course, was that this may be all right in a perfect world, but it is highly idealistic in a world

2. Leander E. Keck, General Editor, *New Interpreter's Bible* (Nashville: Abingdon Press, 1994), I:464.

3. Ibid., I:465.

that doesn't have a great deal of respect for such sentiments. In other words, he responded with a healthy dose of skepticism.

Is that attitude, that spirit, the same when it comes to the interaction between God and people? Are we just as skeptical thinking that God still visits people as the Lord did Sarah and Abraham? We look at the scriptures and are told that God came to Abraham in the form of three messengers. We read stories in which axe heads float and donkeys speak. We hear of angels visiting young maidens and a baby being born without human conception. And, we read of that baby, now a man, bringing sight to the blind, the ability to walk to those who are lame, and even that he brings life to those who are clearly and irrefutably dead. And we believe it; or, if we don't, we don't tell anybody for fear of being branded as heretics.

Yet, we look around us and we hear no voice of God, no angels, no miracles. Does God speak today as the Bible tells us was true in the olden days? Is it still possible that nothing is too wonderful for the Lord? And when we hear of those who offer testimony that, indeed, God has wrought a miracle in their lives, do we laugh as Sarah did?

Consider again the source of her laughter. We have recounted the years of frustration caused by her barrenness, which, of course, in that culture was a clear sign of God's disfavor. We have noted that finally God has come in such a way as to lead Abraham and Sarah to think the Lord is once-and-for-all about to deliver on this long-made promise. We have considered that even then the message is given directly only to Abraham; Sarah has to hear it behind the scenes. We know that at least twice Abraham passed off Sarah as his sister, placing her in very difficult situations, presumably to save his own skin. Think of the pent-up frustration and bitterness that have built up over the years. And then this ridiculous notion that in her ninetieth year she will give birth. It is no wonder she laughed.

But it is almost as if God is saying to her, "Sarah, I'm going to show you just how I do fulfill my promises. I'm going to reveal to you that when it comes to doing what only I can do, nothing—absolutely nothing—is laughable." Can we say the same? Or do we give the final word to cynical radio talk-show hosts?

It seems that if we are to see the footprints of God in our world, and in our individual lives, we have to look pretty hard. And even then, our vision must come through spiritual eyes. Repeatedly, Jesus said, *He who has the eyes to see, let him see.* What did he mean? Perhaps this: miracles today are rarely, if ever, evident to the naked eye. What is a miracle to a child of God might be something else entirely to one who has little or no faith. My guess is that my experience is not unlike yours in that I've seen a miracle or two in my time. But the casual observer might have seen nothing. Let me illustrate . . .

Fred Basgier was the chairman of deacons at Middle River Baptist Church in Baltimore, Maryland when I accepted their call to serve as pastor in 1982. Fred had already had a bout with cancer, and after we moved to Baltimore it reared its ugly head one more time. About a year-and-a-half later Fred was in the hospital dying. In the meantime, he and I had developed a very close relationship, largely through his efforts I must admit. He was a man who knew how to befriend and support his pastor.

Fred was reading his Bible in the hospital one day and came across the passage in James that says, "Are any among you sick? They should call for the elders of the church and have them pray over them, anointing them with oil in the name of the Lord. The prayer of faith will save the sick, and the Lord will raise them up" (5:14-15a). And Fred took it to heart. He asked if I would be willing to gather a few deacons and ministers in the church, come to the hospital, anoint him with oil, and pray for him. Though I had never done this, and haven't since, I would have done just about anything for my friend because I knew he would do the same for me.

Several of us from the church came to his hospital room one evening, and after a short time of visiting, we circled his bed. Fred's wife Katie had brought some olive oil. I took it, put some on my finger, pressed it to his forehead, and prayed for Fred's healing. One-by-one, all the others did the same. It was, as you might imagine, an emotional time for us all as we prayed for our good friend and brother in Christ.

A few weeks later Fred died a slow and agonizing death. After he was gone, Katie and I were visiting together. She knew she could share her grief and hurt and innermost feelings with me. Finally, she confessed to her confusion and anger toward God, that after going to such measures as outlined in the epistle, her husband wasn't healed. My response to her was that perhaps he had been healed. I asked her if she had noticed how agitated Fred was before.

When I visited him he would always be uneasy, and his pain would keep him from being able to concentrate on what we were talking about. But after that night of anointing and prayer, a sense of calm and peace came over him that had not existed before. His spirit had been healed in a way that, obviously, his body had not. And now, in his mercy and grace, God had granted him the ultimate healing by taking Fred to his eternal home.

Is anything too wonderful for the Lord?

By the way, Sarah wasn't the only one who laughed. Abraham laughed too. Earlier in the story, in a portion of scripture that is not cited at the beginning of this chapter, we are told that the Lord said to Abraham that Sarah would be blessed, and even though he is an old man, Abraham would be given a son by her. And the Bible says, "Then Abraham fell on his face and laughed" (17:17). Not politely and behind his hands as Sarah did, but on his face.

Both Sarah and Abraham were skeptical. And they were fearful. *And they were faithful.* It took both of these old people to do God's will, stumbling together, crying together, laughing together. And that is why, despite the miraculous nature of this conception, the story of Sarah and Abraham is really very common, for it is much like your life story and mine. Life is lived to its fullest when we seek God's will, knowing that it is not a clear, nor an easy, proposition. But it does take us to God's final destination.

So I would encourage us all to let Sarah—and Abraham—speak to us. My friends, we journey together toward the kingdom of God. And we do it amidst fear and faith, with tears and great laughter. And maybe, just maybe, it is the laughter that God blesses the most.

REBEKAH

"AT ANY COST"

Let your curse be upon me, my son; only obey my word, and go, get them for me (Genesis 27:13).

Sarah, the wife of Abraham, is now dead and Abraham is old. Abraham has lived for so many years with the promise of God ringing in his ears that it is a permanent and constant part of who he is. It is vitally important, then, that he find the right wife for his son Isaac so God's purpose and blessing can continue. Isaac, you will recall, is the result of God's long held promise that Abraham's descendants would outnumber the stars. So this has to be done right. Too much is riding on it. It has to be done just right.

To ensure that Isaac will have a life partner who will follow the covenantal ways of Yahweh, Abraham centers his search on the land of his fathers. However, the future wife of Isaac must agree to come to Isaac. Under no circumstances is Isaac to return to his father's homeland. It would be a sign of Abraham's rejection of God's purpose to build a new nation of people committed to doing the will of God in a place that God himself will choose. Isaac's wife must come from the homeland, but she also has to agree to leave home, just as Abraham did many years before, never to return. It appears to be a daunting, if not impossible, task to find such a woman.

Have you noticed how often, in the Old Testament scriptures, wives are found at the village well? Lo and behold, the very first young woman who comes to the well is the one!

How lucky can you get? And, according to the customs of that day (and not that much unlike the customs of our own) she has everything going for her: she is kin to Abraham, which, in those days, works in her favor; she is a virgin, and she is beautiful. She is also generous, willing to offer water to Abraham's camels as well as to Eliezer, Abraham's wife-seeking servant. The servant is pleased with this young lady, for he has ten camels and she has only one jar. That's a lot of work, but she is willing to do it. It shows how far she will go to provide hospitality, even to a total stranger. Yes, this Rebekah is going to work out fine, just fine.

God has much invested in this enterprise with Abraham. But God did not create humans to live forever. Abraham is getting on in years. God's concern now is that the covenant he established with Abraham be carried on to the next generation and the next. Will the promise be safely entrusted to those who follow Abraham? Yes, it will, but that doesn't mean it is going to be easy.

As was true with her late mother-in-law Sarah, Rebekah proves to be barren, and for the first twenty years of her marriage to Isaac she is unable to bear children. It is a recurring theme in the biblical narratives that we will see again in the life of Hannah; that such barrenness serves to reveal the miraculous intervention of God. Passing the faith from one generation to the next is not just the natural order of things. It is the intent and purpose of God. However, this part of the story is not as involved as it was with Sarah. We are simply told, "Isaac prayed to the Lord for his wife, because she was barren; and the Lord granted his prayer, and his wife Rebekah conceived" (Genesis 25:21). That's it. No waiting years and years until old age sets in. No messengers of God. No babies born in the geriatric wing. Rebekah's story has its twists and turns, but they are revealed in other ways, ways that are just as intriguing, if not more so.

There are other differences in Rebekah's story from that of Sarah, very important differences. God chose to reveal his plan for Sarah only by means of communicating with Abraham. Whatever Sarah learned of God's plan for her life, she discovered secondhand. With Rebekah, God speaks directly. In fact, it seems that God goes out of his way not to communicate with Isaac. Is that a reflection of Rebekah's personal strength and faith, or is it a commentary on Isaac's weakness? Perhaps, as we shall see, it is both.

With today's medical technology, expectant parents can be told the gender of their children fairly early in the process of the pregnancy. Well, they've got nothing on Rebekah! She needs no such help. She receives the news directly from God, almost in poetic form . . .

Two nations are in your womb,
and two peoples born of you shall be divided;
the one shall be stronger than the other,
the elder shall serve the younger (25:23).

Rebekah has conceived twins. And God has a plan that is to cause extreme difficulty for this budding family of four. Their experiences reveal that God has always chosen to reveal the divine plan strictly in the Lord's own way. It may seem strange and inexplicable to us, but we can't argue with the results, can we? Nevertheless, though we know God hardly has to explain it to us, we can't help but wonder why the Lord would want to use and bless such rascally people!

In Rebekah's story, interestingly enough, the power of blessing is revealed; yet, the blessing, or birthright, is procured through the practice of deceit and cunning. If nothing else, it ought to give us hope that, if God is willing to use and bless people like this, there might be hope for us! But what kind of blessing is it? And is a blessing gotten by deception still a blessing? As far as we can determine, the power to which the blessing points is found in the words of the blessing itself. It is ironic that the spoken blessing, which is to be the agent of peace that binds generations together in purpose and faith, becomes instead the instrument of division and suffering. Jacob has to run for his life, Esau is filled with hatred, Isaac is left to stew in his blind impotence, unable to make right what he considers to be a great wrong, and Rebekah is left with a crumbled, separated, and bitter family. God does indeed have a strange sense of blessing, isn't that true?

Why doesn't Rebekah simply tell her husband Isaac what God has said? Perhaps she considers just that. But she knows Isaac has a special relationship with Esau, just as she does with Jacob. He may very well not believe her that God spoke to her in such a direct and personal way. After all, when God chose to communicate with his parents, the message always came to his father Abraham, not his mother Sarah. If God had a message for his family, why wouldn't the Lord talk to him? Why would God talk to Rebekah instead? That line of reasoning does seem more consistent with the way God has operated in the past, doesn't it? By the time Isaac comes into the biblical picture, the practice of patriarchy is deeply entrenched. It just doesn't make sense, at least in that day and time, that God would speak to a woman.

Early on, we get a picture of Rebekah as this sweet, demure, generous, thoughtful, and beautiful young maiden. However, let's not forget from whence she has come. Rebekah is introduced to us by the writer of Genesis as the daughter of Bethuel, son of Milcah, the wife of Nahor, who was Abraham's brother. And, she is the sister of Laban. Does that name *Laban* ring a bell? He is prominent in the continuing story and it is necessary to tell some of that story for us to have a better understanding of Rebekah's psyche.

Laban would later become the father of daughters, Leah and Rachel. When Jacob flees the wrath of his brother Esau over stealing his father's birthright, he runs to Abraham's homeland. It is there he discovers his cousin Rachel. She too is beautiful. Evidently, beauty runs in the family! Jacob falls immediately in love, but is tricked by Laban into marrying the older, and possibly dowdier, sister Leah. Because of Laban's trickery, Jacob must work fourteen long years before he secures the hand of his beloved Rachel. The relationship between Jacob and Laban, who is both his father-in-law and his uncle, reads like a chess match. They are constantly trying to outwit the other, whether it has to do with the choice of wives or the securing of wealth. Deception, as well as beauty, runs all through this family, doesn't it? As they say, the hen always comes back to roost, and Rebekah's "roosting place" is the henhouse of deception. She goes to great measure to trick her husband and her firstborn son. It just seems to come naturally.

What in the world would cause a wife and mother to do such a thing? Doesn't she understand the anger that would ensue? Does she not care that hatred would become an awesome barrier between her twin sons? What is going on in the conniving mind and heart of Rebekah?

Talk about a dysfunctional family! It is worth noting that Jacob and Esau never appear together in this part of the story, nor do Rebekah and Esau. Their alienation from one another is already complete. The stage is set for Rebekah to do her thing.

Economists tell us that in this current generation the largest amount of personal wealth in the history of the world is being transferred to the baby boomers from their parents. In today's world, generally an inheritance is left to all the children in equal amounts. But in biblical times, especially early on as is true in the Book of Genesis, the birthright is not just an inheritance. It is far more important than that; important enough that it dominates this story and preoccupies the time and intentions of Rebekah. The blessing involves the earlier promise God had given to Abraham, a promise that is about to be given to the third generation.

Divine in nature, the blessing is the spoken word of God that literally shapes the destiny of human life. Would it be given to the bright and cunning Jacob or to Esau the dolt? The birthright is both riches and Godly favor. It is the most important thing in all the world, and was reserved for the eldest son. But Rebekah will do anything—anything—to see that her favorite son Jacob is the one who receives it. In fact, when Jacob protests her plan, not because he thinks it's wrong but because he does not believe it will work, his mother Rebekah assumes all the responsibility of the consequences. That's wanting it awfully badly, isn't it?

Those of you who know this story, who have been familiar with it for many years, what is your reaction to all this? The tendency is to feel sorry for Esau, despite the fact that he appears to be either too stupid or too undisciplined to deserve his father's blessing. Not only that, but going against the expressed wishes of his father and his God, Esau takes two Canaanite women for wives, creating great discord between them and Rebekah. None of these characters seems to be able to do anything right . . . or righteous. Yet, our sympathy still turns away from Rebekah and Jacob for their duplicity and deception. Is that basically the way you feel about this situation?

On the surface, Rebekah seems to be nothing short of a selfish schemer. She wants the blessing for Jacob because Jacob is her favorite son. And we all know the terrible tragedy that can result when parents or other family members develop favoritism such as this.

However, Hebrew tradition obviously holds Rebekah in high esteem. According to the tradition, Rebekah was a woman even the forces of nature respected. The sages say that when she went to draw water from a well she did not have to bend over far and reach into its depths to fill her water jar. Rather, the level of the water would rise so she could fill her container with ease.*

Why is the scheming Rebekah loved so much? Perhaps it is this: Unlike Sarah, Rebekah has been given a mission straight from God. She is to see to it, according to God's instructions, that the birthright will be given to Jacob, not Esau. Despite tradition, it seems that God has a plan all worked out and Rebekah is to be the instrument of the Lord's will. Whatever it takes to get the job done, so be it. Rebekah's gifts do not lie in the ability to deal with her husband Isaac on the basis of reason or straightforwardness, or even persuasion. He is now an old blind man, who seems to be as insensitive and unresponsive as his elder son Esau. All the sweet nothings whispered in his ear will be to no avail. Besides, that isn't Rebekah's strong suit anyway. It is in her blood, it is simply her nature, to get what she wants by means of deception. If that includes deceiving her husband and elder son, so be it. Whatever it takes to get the job done, that is what Rebekah will do, and God has told her explicitly what God wants done.

We tend to think that the deception and lies and trickery are the real stars in this story, but perhaps it is time for us to rethink what the writer of Genesis is telling us. The main point is that God tells Rebekah what is to be done, and she is willing to do it regardless of the cost. Amazingly, she is also prepared to sacrifice her family life in the bargain. She alienates Esau, her elder son, and she loses her beloved son Jacob when he has to flee the wrath of his brother. Her deception, rather than just a character flaw, can be viewed as an act of great faith and devotion toward her God. As strange as it seems to us, that is what this fascinating story reveals. Rebekah puts the purposes of God before the welfare of her family or

* Michael E. Williams, editor, *The Storyteller's Companion to the Bible: Old Testament Women*, Vol. 4 (Nashville: Abingdon Press, 1993), p. 3.

herself. What faith!

It is very rare that the ends justify the means, even if the end is a worthy one. But this story just may be the exception. And, it reveals that more often than not, faith—real and true faith—is often lived out in the midst of the rawness and sinfulness of life. God seems to be willing to take the human creation, that is, you and me, and use us according to the Lord's purpose. Rather than making sure we are up to the task and that we are worthy in meeting this lofty standard before we are chosen, God takes us as we are in the hope that our faith experiences will enable us to at least begin to be something of who God is. And every once in awhile, God surely finds someone who has a Rebekah kind of faith.

What does it take to have a Rebekah faith? Not the deception and trickery, but the willingness to do anything to accomplish God's will?

Considering a biblical narrative such as this does little good if we do not inject ourselves into the story. What do the experiences of Rebekah and her family tell us in regard to our faith journey? Perhaps that lesson begins with a question. To what measure will we go to do God's will? And when you think of God's will, what do you think it is? Not for somebody else, but for you?

With regard to the issue of God's will, you may go through your entire lifetime without hearing what you consider to be the voice of God. We don't know how God chose to speak to Rebekah, but we doubt, frankly, that God will speak to us in such a way that we are absolutely, absolutely, convinced; at least to the point that we respond at the level Rebekah did. But this is what we can do: live our lives with a consistent faith, doing day-by-day what we think is right, based on the guidance we are given through scripture, through prayer, and the fellowship of Christ and his church. Then, in those rare and crucial moments when we are called upon to make an important, and possibly life-changing, decision, we do it . . . without questioning, without hesitation, and without looking back. Through the diligence of our daily faith that led us to that point, we trust that God is with us, and we do what we feel God wants us to do.

And, like our sister Rebekah, we do it at any cost.

MIRIAM

"THE SINGER"

Then the prophet Miriam, Aaron's sister, took a tambourine in her hand; and all the women went out after her with tambourines and with dancing (Exodus 15:10).

In the spring of 1912 four young women met for a time of prayer in Arkansas' capital city of Little Rock. They had a particular concern. They felt it was time a church was started in the area of town called Hillcrest. First populated by those of financial means who used this area for their summer retreats, Hillcrest was now the end of the streetcar line. Such public conveyance meant that Hillcrest had become a neighborhood conducive to permanent, year-round homes. People were living there full-time, raising families, living out their faith. By the time the second decade of the twentieth century rolled around, there were quite a few folk in this part of town who called themselves Baptist. The other Baptist churches, in the estimation of these good women, were too far away, given the condition of the city's streets and the fact that it was 1912 and, despite the streetcars, it wasn't so easy to get around in those days. Hillcrest was growing rapidly and deserved its own church. From that first meeting came the Pulaski Heights Baptist congregation.

Not only did these young women keep faith with good Baptist tradition in following their dream, they also found precedence in the scriptures; not the least of which is the story from the Book of Exodus that depicts Miriam, the sister of Moses. We are taught many things in scripture, and one of them is that major events—even turning-the-world-upside-down events—often begin with the smallest of deeds. Just by praying and sharing their concerns, these four women began a movement that led to the formation of a thriving church.

It is doubtful these young women had the story of baby Moses in mind when they met, but you never know, you just never know. It, too, is an example of this important lesson; namely, that the biggest things can come from what, at the time, don't seem to amount to very much at all. Through the actions of four women—two Hebrew and two Egyptian—God's people were liberated and the nation of Israel was to be given birth. Let's consider the background.

The Hebrews have been in Egypt four hundred years. At first, they were welcomed by the Egyptians, for they were descended from Joseph, who had come to be trusted and beloved by the Egyptian leadership. But, as the Book of Exodus tells us, there eventually came to power a Pharaoh "who knew not Joseph." He has no memory of the good role the Hebrews played in earlier generations, and so he enslaves God's people. They become subjected by the Pharaoh to oppression and dehumanizing labor. They become victims of genocide and are treated like dogs.

Because the Hebrews continue to multiply in numbers,

and in the mind of the paranoid Pharaoh, represent a threat to his peoples' well-being, he issues a decree that all male infants are to be killed at birth by the Hebrew midwives. When that doesn't succeed to his satisfaction, he tells his own people that if they find any Hebrew male babies, they are to throw them into the River Nile. It is during this period of time that our story begins to unfold.

But before we go any further with the story, let's consider something essential about those whose lives are central to this exciting narrative. There comes a point in life when we must assume responsibility for our own actions, Sigmund Freud notwithstanding. Nevertheless, it cannot be denied that who we are, and certain traits we exhibit, come down from those who brought us into the world and parented us. Those with stubborn streaks might prefer to think of it as dogged determination, but they are probably just as quick to blame it on Mom or Dad. And we can't deny that certain mannerisms find their origin in those who brought us into the world and raised us. It is simply inevitable.

It was just as inevitable for Moses and his big sister Miriam. Imagine, if you will, the courage, the strength and stubbornness (or is that dogged determination?) it took for their mother to defy the Pharaoh, the most important leader in that part of the world. To keep her male child was a supreme act of subversion, and if found out would surely have resulted in her death and the deaths of all her family members. This was a violent time, and mercy was not a strong suit in those days.

In Owen Wister's 1902 novel, *The Virginian*, a story of the Old West, the Virginian's friend Steve has been caught rustling cattle. Steve is well liked, not only by the hero of the story, but by every one who knows him. But, when he is caught red-handed, he is hanged just like the rest of the renegades in his gang. Adding to the complexity of the situation is the fact that, unlike some of the others, he dies very bravely. The Virginian, of course, is deeply saddened by his friend's death, but he is also aware that, while justice can be brutal, that's simply the way it is in the rugged west.

That was even truer in Egypt. Mercy was not plentiful in Egypt, and at the time of our story, the guys who wore the black hats were in charge. From the biblical perspective, their violence was not based on justice, however, but on fear. They were afraid the Hebrews would come to outnumber them, and therefore the Hebrews formed a great threat to the well-being of their people.

The mother of Moses and Miriam knows the rules, despicable as they may be. If she gets caught, she and all her family would face the Egyptian equivalent of a rope. Yet, she is willing to defy Pharaoh and then give up her son to the vagaries of fate. It appears that she is motivated either by great faith or great fear. Regardless of which it is, she will be blessed because of her actions.

Moses is three months old. The writer of Exodus says about the mother of Moses, "When she could hide him no longer . . ."

This story took on new meaning for me when my first grandson was born. By the time Alex reached the age of three months, I delighted in observing how he had taken over the emotions, not to mention the activities, of an entire family. That joy was compounded by noting his mother's obvious love for this little guy with the quick and delightful laugh. I enjoyed witnessing the depths of her devotion to him. Do you know why Moses's mother could hide him no longer? I'll tell you why. At the age of three months, my grandson had learned how to laugh and talk and make all kinds of sounds. And on those occasions when he was unhappy, he made his feelings equally known loud and clear!

Surely, though it was obviously a different day and time, that is much like it was with Moses. It is the same kind of bonding that took place between this Hebrew mother and her son. Noise and laughter filled the household, but to their great peril. So what does the mother of Moses do? She puts him in a basket and sets him afloat! Imagine! The River Nile, made red with the blood of the Hebrew babies, will give back the leader who will free his people from their oppression. And all because this woman was willing to take such a risk!

And then Miriam comes into the story. There is no indication in the scriptures that Miriam observes her baby brother because her mother has given her orders to do so. According to the way the story is told, she simply does it. Very soon she is given the opportunity to use her wits in preserving, not only his life, but in keeping intact the contact and relationship between her mother and her mother's infant. Chip off the old block!

The infant has been found by the Pharaoh's daughter and her maidservant. Miriam steps in and suggests that the baby will need a nursemaid. Should she go and find a Hebrew woman to do what the princess cannot do, and probably wouldn't want to do? She brings her mother to the princess, who obviously doesn't see the family resemblance, and the princess gives her instructions to care for the baby. It is interesting, is it not, that though the Hebrews had been enslaved by the Egyptians, the princess offers wages to the baby's mother.

On the surface of things, it could appear to be simply an interchange among four women, just as in 1912 it might have seemed that four women of Hillcrest simply got together for a chat. But what Miriam did that day began a string of events that would eventually lead to the freedom of the Israelites, the rejuvenation of God's people as a nation, and change the history of the world forever. And it all began with a simple question: "Shall I go and get you a nurse from the Hebrew women to nurse the child for you?"

It is true, isn't it? You just never know what major events are begun by the smallest of deeds. That simple, but clever, question began the inexorable process of shutting down the violence perpetrated by the Egyptians against Miriam's people, and became the catalyst for the freedom of an entire nation.

Every child in Sunday School is fascinated by the story of the rescue of baby Moses from the waters of the Nile, and why not? It has intrigue, violence, and human compassion. Children are filled with wonder, and not a small sense of terror, that such cruelty can be wrought against defenseless babies. The same emotion is found when we consider Herod's slaughter of the innocents during Jesus' early childhood. And while the women are prominent in this story—there's no way to get around it, even if you wanted to—how often is the story considered from the women's perspective?

As we've noted, Moses's mother defies the Pharaoh and nurtures her infant son until that fateful day she puts him in the little makeshift boat and sets him adrift. Why did his sister Miriam stand, as the Bible says, "at a distance, to see what would happen to him"? Morbid curiosity? Not likely! And why Miriam? Could her mother not bear to see her baby's fate?

Think again of the courage it took for Miriam to do what she did. As is often the case, the Bible tells the story in understated terms. Because the Bible is not written as a novel, it does not reveal the emotions involved. So, we find ourselves having to read between the lines. But, is it not true that this is where most of the fun originates in studying scripture: taking the biblical story, and with the use of our God-given imaginations, filling it in with our own thoughts and ideas and understandings, as limited as they may be sometimes? Let's see where this kind of exercise will take us.

The chances are Miriam has never before spoken to an Egyptian. She is a Hebrew slave girl, and all Egyptians were their captors, their enemies. And even if she has spoken to an Egyptian, certainly she has never talked with one who has the stature of the Pharaoh's daughter. Yet, she musters up the resolve to do so. There is simply too much at stake.

Do you think, as she steps forward to speak to the princess, that she is considering the future of her people? Do you think she is pondering how this would be the beginning of their liberation? Do you think she considers her importance in the history of Israel? Of course not. No more than the Apostle Paul sat down to write a letter and thought to himself, "I think I'll write some scripture today." No, she is thinking of only one thing: protecting her baby brother, securing the welfare of her family, and doing what it would take to insure that the ultimate grief would not be visited on her household.

It is not stated, but is implied, that God is quietly using young Miriam to fulfill the divine will in the fate of God's children Israel. It is time for the rescue of God's own people. It is indeed true that such a tremendous event as the Hebrew exodus from Egypt would begin with the courage of a mother, and come to fruition by means of a young girl who dared ask a question. "Shall I go and get you a nurse?" It is funny how God works, isn't it?

Speaking of God . . . God isn't mentioned much in this story. In fact, God isn't mentioned at all. Why do you think that is?

The Hebrews, as we mentioned, have been in Egypt for more than four centuries, and they are now enslaved. Can you imagine the constant sense of chaos, destruction, and death that hangs over God's chosen people? If you have ever fought in a war, perhaps you can; or struggled with poverty, or dealt with a life threatening illness . . . Hope tends to play out over the course of time, does it not? If God is alive, then God has a strange way of showing it. Where is Abraham's promise? Did the ancient Sarah secure Abraham's lineage only for the children of God to suffer in slavery in a land that is not their own? Was Rebekah's scheming to no avail?

It might very well be that, from the Hebrews' viewpoint, their God has become an absentee God. And then, in the midst of their despair, comes a brave Hebrew mother, followed by an equally courageous daughter. In keeping with that family tradition, a son has been born—a son who, by fate, grows up with that same, courageous spirit to lead his people to freedom and liberty. And as this story unfolds, we discover, slowly but surely, it isn't fate at all which is responsible for the outcome. God is very much aware of the plight of his people, and is beginning to weave the divine purpose into their destiny.

While God may be hidden, the unnamed sister of Moses, Miriam we are to find out later, is very active in saving her baby brother. She is the instrument by which God will have God's will done in the lives of the people Israel. There is no fate involved here. We find an active God who watches and cares for God's people, a loving God who lets the story unfold according to the divine timetable. And while we might think it is overstated, it cannot be denied that the fate of God's children rests in the quick thinking actions of Moses's sister, Miriam, to see that her baby brother survives the paranoid frenzy of the Pharaonic slave driver.

The scene now shifts, and it is years later. Moses leads his people out of Egypt and to the edge of the Red Sea. Not only is the Pharaoh paranoid, he is fickle to boot. After agreeing to let the Israelites go free, he changes his mind and pursues them. Has God led them out of slavery to this, a watery grave? No, of course not. The sea is parted and the Hebrew people cross on dry land. And as the Egyptian armies pursue them across the dry seabed, the waters return and it is the oppressors who are buried in the depths of the sea, drowned in their own savagery.

Notice who leads the celebration: Miriam! And what is her message? Does she pay homage to her brother Moses, whose freedom she secured years before when he was an infant? Does she sing praises to her mother, who was so brave in securing the life of her infant son? No. Her praise is given to Yahweh, the God of Israel, who has made Israel free . . .

> *Sing to the* LORD, *for he has triumphed gloriously;*
> *horse and rider he has thrown into the sea.*

Miriam is leading her people to affirm that God is not asleep. If the Lord had ever been asleep, Yahweh, God of Abraham, Isaac, and Jacob, is now alive! God leads Israel from treachery back to the promise. And no one has more right to direct the people in worship than Miriam, the singer and prophet, whose quick actions so many years before began the process of salvation for her people.

Compared to other women in the scriptures, Miriam appears to have only a cameo appearance. Once the story is told of how she used her wits in securing her mother as a nursemaid for the Egyptian princess, she becomes overshadowed by that same younger brother and her other brother Aaron. It fits what her life's story tell us. Major events, even those experiences which change the course of our world's history, often begin with the smallest of deeds and involve people who, by the world's standards, seem insignificant. After all, think of the One born of a peasant woman in a tiny, obscure village, who never traveled very far from home, never knew a king, and never had any wealth. Yet, through his life of sacrificial giving, and through his willingness to take upon himself the wrath of the world, he has turned the world upside down, and the world has never since been the same.

If you have ever wondered how God works in the lives of his human creation, look no further than that. And consider that God might just want to weave his will in your life in much the same manner. No fanfare, and maybe not even goose bumps.

As always, when we leave this story and other stories of faith found in the scriptures, the journey continues to await us. As you travel, look for the smallest of things, the mustard seeds of life, and in them you might just find the presence and purpose of God. And when you do, remember Miriam. In your own way, take up the timbrel and dance. "Sing to the LORD, for he has triumphed gloriously." The Lord has triumphed indeed.

RUTH

"WHITHERSOEVER"

Do not press me to leave you or to turn back from following you! Where you go, I will go; where you lodge, I will lodge; your people shall be my people, and your God my God (Ruth 1:16).

In the far northeast reaches of rural Greene County, Arkansas, nestled against the Missouri boot heel line, you will find the vestiges of a rather once-thriving little community called Epsaba. At one time, my ancestors on my mother's side lived in the small clapboard tin-roofed homes that dotted the flat landscape of that little part of the world.

Their names were Green and Rogers, Stone and Cole, Throgmartin and Glenn. They were hardly wealthy. In fact, descended from people who had largely tended the earth and put meager crops in it, by today's economic standards they were quite poor; which is why, after the Second World War was ended, and the automobile industry once again began producing automobiles rather than airplanes for the war effort, many of the residents of Epsaba migrated north to Michigan in order to work the assembly lines. And that is why so many of them, like my late Uncle Pete and Cousin Jerry, Aunt Imogene and Cousin Sandra, always talked "funny." Even my Uncle Chester Cole, married to my mother's older sister, Bea, left his home country. You see, he pastored the Epsaba Baptist Church, and since his congregation went north, he decided to go with them.

They were all seeking survival, which puts them in pretty good company. If you have read John Grisham's novel, *The Painted House*, you will find my extended family's story told within those pages.

In the days when the Hebrew judges ruled over the Israelites, roughly twelve hundred years before Christ, a famine came to the region of Bethlehem. That, in itself, is painfully ironic since the name *Bethlehem* means "house of bread." The family of Elimelek escapes the famine by migrating to the land of the Moabites. And while it is tempting for me to think of this story simply in terms of my family moving from Arkansas to Michigan following the big war, there is a bit more involved in this story than just that.

The Old Testament narrative identifies the family as "Ephrathites." Ephratha is the old name for Bethlehem, and reveals that the family of Elimelek may have been one of the old guard, indigenous families of Bethlehem . . . the upper crust, if you will, if there was such a thing in those parts and in those days. In other words, it would be like the Rockefellers having to flee and migrate.[1] It must have been a really desperate time.

Desperate times call for desperate measures, and Elimelek, well-known aristocrat though he may have been, decides not to ride out the famine but to go to a land that

1. Ellen van Wolde, *Ruth and Naomi* (Macon: Smyth & Helwys, 1998), p. 9.

promises greater prosperity. Perhaps he likes living well, and the prospect of having to grub for a living doesn't appeal to him. He hears that things are going well in Moab, so Moab it shall be.

However, Moab only brings hardship and death. We are told very quickly in the story that Elimelek dies. The two sons of Elimelek and his wife Naomi, Mahlon and Chilion, hardly take their two wives from the Moabite women before they too die. Three people remain: Naomi and her two daughters-in-law, Orpah and Ruth.

If today, we were to hear that a woman had been widowed, then lost both her sons—her only children—we would, of course, be saddened for her. It is a shame that someone has to bear these kinds of losses. However, in the days of Naomi it was more than just a shame; it was absolutely devastating. We are told, "the woman was left without her two sons and her husband." That statement is packed with all kinds of meaning, meaning which is tied up in the strange culture of that day. It is also packed with pathos, and its implication is central to this entire story. "The woman was left without her two sons and her husband."

It was, some thirty-two hundred years ago, most definitely a man's world. In a marriage relationship, the woman was the husband's property, and found her fulfillment and purpose in life through her husband. Her identity was defined by the fact that she was "So-and-So, daughter of So-and-So," or "wife of So-and-So," or "sister of So-and-So." And when these men disappear, her identity disappears too. That is exactly what happened to Naomi, widow of Elimelek and mother of the late Mahlon and Chilion.

If your name is Ruth, and you live with your mother-in-law Naomi, who has lost her husband and her two sons, then you are a nobody attached to a nobody. Ruth has what we would call a double whammy.

Why was this so? The clue is found in an expression used often in scripture, especially in the Old Testament, that is often overlooked. Sometimes the plainest statements in scripture yield a mother lode of understanding and background if we can just dig beneath them. That is true here. Often you will read that a certain man married a certain woman. At least, that's the way we interpret it. Actually, it does not say that a certain man married a certain woman. We are informed that a certain man *took* a certain woman for his wife, and that is a big difference.

The idea of marriage, two people becoming one by means of the ritual of taking vows, follows a number of years after this story occurred. This doesn't mean we are not talking about a lifelong relationship. It means the relationship is not equal. The woman is tied exclusively to the man, for he has *taken* her, but the man is not tied exclusively to the woman. He can *take* other wives for himself. So when he is out of the picture, the wife is left alone to her own devices. If she is advanced in years, it can only be hoped she has produced male sons who will take care of her in her old age.

Naomi and Ruth are in a world of hurt. Neither is survived by a male who will take responsibility for their well-being. They are women without, adrift on the sea with no oar. It just doesn't get any worse than this.

Recognizing their plight, Naomi implores Orpah and Ruth to go back home. It is too late for her, but perhaps they can find husbands among their own people. As for her, she's going home. It won't be easy, but it would be better than staying in a foreign land. Her argument makes sense to Orpah, and she returns, evidently to see if she can find another man who will *take* her as his wife.

But Ruth remains, and in the course of her conversation with Naomi, she utters these words of commitment that still ring in our ears today, after all these years:

Do not press me to leave you or to turn back from following you!
Where you go, I will go;
Where you lodge, I will lodge;
your people shall be my people, and your God, my God.
Where you die, I will die—
there will I be buried. . . .

Perhaps you prefer, and are more familiar with, the King James Version:

Intreat me not to leave thee, or to return from following after thee:
for whither thou goest, I will go;
and where thou lodgest, I will lodge:
thy people shall be my people, and thy God my God.

Fred Craddock tells of the time he was visiting in New York and went to the Riverside Church where James Forbes was pastor. Dr. Forbes used as his sermon text the New Testament reading from Luke 9 where the man tells Jesus, "Lord, I will follow thee whithersoever thou goest" (v. 57). He began his sermon this way: "Whithersoever. Whithersoever. Whithersoever. Whithersoever. Whithersoever." Dr. Craddock said he thought at first this was going to be the only word he would utter during the entire sermon. "Whithersoever." Of course, his purpose was to *burn* the word into the minds and hearts of his listeners, so they would take it with them, and in the process know the depth and meaning of following Jesus at any cost. "Whithersoever."

It is that same level of commitment that Ruth gives her mother-in-law Naomi. And she receives from Naomi pretty much the same response Jesus gives the man who makes such a bold affirmation of discipleship. *Foxes have holes, and birds of the air have nests; but the Son of Man has nowhere to lay his head.* "Turn back . . ." Naomi says to Ruth, "it has been far more bitter for me than for you . . . the hand of the Lord has turned against me." Do you get the sense that Naomi is disappointed in, and not a little bit angry with, God?

"Turn back." "Turn back." For Ruth to cast her future with Naomi, a three-time loser, is for her a losing enterprise as well. Naomi has no future and no prospects of support. "The hand of the Lord has turned against me." She may be going back home, but she has shuttered up her life and won't let anyone, even Ruth or God, come in. That often happens to people when they experience deep trauma.

A deacon in one of my previous churches was a veteran of World War II. He was a survivor of the famous Bataan Death March and, for almost three years, was a prisoner of war at the hands of the Chinese. It was a horrible experience and many of his comrades died from malnutrition or physical abuse. For fifty years he would not, or could not, talk of his experiences. He had numerous artifacts, as well as pictures, from the war, but he kept them put away. In 1995, during the fiftieth celebration of the ending of the war, he began to talk. A newspaper article was written about him and one of his fellow prisoners who was from the same area. It was almost as if that fifty-year mark closed the psychological wounds that had kept him silenced for half a century. The shutters came off, the bonds were loosed.

Naomi's wounds are still fresh and the shutters remain. In fact, when she returns to her hometown of Bethlehem, the women who have not seen her in years, ask, "Is this Naomi?" "No," she replies, "Call me no longer Naomi, call me *Mara*." The name Naomi means "pleasant" or "lovely," but as far as she is concerned that is no longer her name. Her name is now Mara. *Mara* means "bitter." That is now her name: *Bitter*. "Turn back," she tells her daughter-in-law. "Turn back. Let me wallow in my bitterness alone." But Ruth won't take "No" for an answer. "She gives up everything without knowing what she will get back in return."[2]

There is no indication whatsoever that Naomi appreciates Ruth's magnanimous gesture or is grateful for her devotion. There is nothing in the story to give us the idea that she even thanks her daughter-in-law for the companionship. "She said no more to her," the story tells us. "She said no more to her." A shrug of the shoulders, and in silence she starts the bitter journey back to Judah with Ruth trailing behind.

With our twenty-first century sensitivities, it is difficult for us to understand this kind of blind allegiance. And believe it, it is *blind* allegiance. After all, Ruth adopts Naomi's God, but not because of Naomi's evangelistic efforts. The only feeling Naomi has toward God is bitterness and anger. Ruth isn't just patronizing her mother-in-law; she is defying the customs and social structure that, in all likelihood, will condemn her

2. Ibid., p. 23.

to being a non-entity in a foreign land which distrusts and despises her. She seems to have everything to lose and nothing to gain. Knowing all this—still knowing all this—she picks up her bag and says, "Let's go."

In a world that is filled with all manner of wrong allegiances and enticing deities, how can we, without the foresight we so tightly cling to and seem to need before moving into the unknown future, rise to this level of commitment? *That* is the key question rising out of this unique biblical story. In other words, how do we commit ourselves to Jesus on the same level Ruth committed herself to Naomi?

Maybe we don't. Maybe we can't. Maybe we aren't willing to take the plunge without a safety net, to say in all respects, "Yes, Lord, I will follow you." But if we are not, Christ died in vain for us. If we are not willing to follow him, God's promise to us remains unfulfilled.

If you know the rest of this intriguing story, you are aware that Ruth meets Naomi's kinsman, Boaz, and eventually Boaz *takes* her to be his wife. Naomi's hope in God is restored and we are told the general feeling in Bethlehem is that Ruth's love for her mother-in-law is worth more than seven sons. Ruth and Boaz have a son named Obed, who will be the grandfather of David, the great king of Israel. Out of great faith comes great reward.

We could almost say, "And they lived happily ever after." But this is not a fairy tale. It is a hard-nosed, realistic story of people who take what life gives them, and out of a mixture of bitterness and hope, tragedy and faith, discover that real security comes only when they are willing to take a risk.

What are we willing to risk? Remember Y2K, the non-event that had so many people scurrying to fill their pantry with rations and withdraw all their money from the bank? That's the world we live in. What does that say about our level of faith? Our planning calendars are guarded like Fort Knox, Caller ID wards off unwanted telephone calls, and our doors are double-bolted. Security is the name of the game. We take no risks when it comes to our physical well-being. Understandably so. But are we willing to take a risk when it comes to our faith?

Perhaps this is the perfect time for us to ask these hard questions. And as we seek to answer them, I would encourage you to consider Ruth. See in your mind's eye this young woman picking up her belongings and following silently the bitter form of her mother-in-law. She travels to an unknown destiny and is willing to accept whatever God holds in store. Can we do the same? Will we? The answer is in our hands and in our hearts.

HANNAH

"The Meaning of Sacrifice"

For this child I prayed; and the Lord has granted me the petition that I made to him. Therefore I have lent him to the Lord; as long as he lives, he is given to the Lord (1 Samuel 1:27-28).

In the movie, *The End,* Burt Reynolds, who is very well cast, plays the part of a fairly pathetic fellow who, near the conclusion of the story, decides to end his life by drowning himself in the Pacific Ocean. We see, from his perspective, the water enveloping him as he sinks deeper and deeper into the sea. Very soon the water will fill his lungs and it will be, indeed, the end. Suddenly, he bursts through the surface of the sea and screams aloud, "I want to live! I want to live!" Then, he realizes just how far from shore he has drifted and he is not certain he has the strength to make it back. So he begins to bargain with God.

"Lord, if you let me live I'll give you ninety percent of everything I make." The closer he gets to the beach, however, the more the percentage decreases . . . from ninety percent to fifty to forty to thirty, and on and on. Finally, when he staggers to his feet safely on *terra firma*, he says, "Well, Lord, if you don't want any of my money, then I won't give it to you."

Bargaining with God. Foxhole prayers. "Lord, if you will do what I ask, I will do such and such in return." "Lord, if you let my child live I will go to church every Sunday." "Lord, if you let me get this job . . . or this promotion . . . or win the lottery . . . or a date with that gorgeous hunk named Mike." Have you ever made a bargain with God? The chances are, in some shape or form, we all have made our deals with the Almighty.

At the beginning of our story about Hannah, a woman who made a deal with God, Israel has evolved into a pathetic nation filled with moral chaos and limited leadership. The Philistines are constantly knocking at her gate, and it isn't because they want to come in and play "Welcome Wagon." Once again, as God did in intervening with Sarah and Abraham, as God did when Israel was brought out of the bondage of Egyptian slavery, God is preparing, ever so slowly and with great patience, to restore God's children to their rightful place in the world. And once again, God does so by responding to the heart-breaking pleas of a barren woman who is desperate enough to make a deal with her God. Sound familiar?

Of course, we know that even this will not be the last time God restores Israel as a fallen people. It is amazing, isn't it, how God is willing, over and over, to begin again with these disobedient and sinful people called Israel. Patience is, indeed, one of God's eternal virtues.

The focus is upon Hannah, wife of Elkanah. She is bitter over her barren plight, so she strikes her deal with God. If God chooses to respond in her favor and grant her a son, she promises that the level of her gratitude will match, and perhaps even surpass, her bitterness. She backs up her promise with a Nazarite vow.

It is not that unusual, of course, for a woman not to be able to bear a child. It can be emotionally traumatic, of course, especially if she desperately wants one, and most of us know someone in that situation. Hence, the medical and scientific breakthroughs of recent years in regard to in vitro fertilization and other forms of artificial means of conception. In the days of Hannah and Elkanah, however, the repercussions of barrenness go far beyond anything we witness today. We have considered this recurring theme already in our discussions of Sarah and Rebekah. To be without children, especially male children, was to be incomplete. It was a sign of God's disfavor and judgment.

The Old Testament, interestingly enough, is not hesitant in waxing theological in this matter. It isn't simply that Hannah has not been able to have children. And we know it has nothing to do with Elkanah, her husband, since he has children by his other wife, Peninnah. The narrator says, "The Lord had closed her womb." This is not just a physiological situation. God has a purpose in all this, according to the chronicler, and God alone, at the beginning of our narrative, knows how the story will unfold.

That may be bothersome to you: the idea that God closed Hannah's womb because the Lord had a purpose in mind. Is she just a puppet for God to play with as God chooses? It seems the least God could have done was to let her in on it, somehow convey to her that there would be years of barrenness before she would be able to produce children. Why not come to Hannah and tell her to be patient, remind her of Sarah, tell her God has a plan in mind? But, no, God is silent and lets her suffer. Only when she comes and makes her deal does God finally deliver. Is that a problem for you? I admit it is for me, or obviously I wouldn't have raised the issue.

If someone in our church desperately wanted a child and was unable to do so, for whatever reason, and I visited with that person and said it is the will of God, what kind of response do you think I would receive? Resentment? Anger? Not only that, but I could rightfully be accused of practicing poor biblical theology. Yet, is that not consistent with what Hannah's story tells us?

If someone has terminal cancer and I suggest that God has caused this in order for that person's faith to be a witness to others suffering from the same condition, do you think it would make that person feel better? No! It would be a terrible, personal intrusion into his or her life, and would cast God in a mean and spiteful light.

Yet, we are told that God has closed Hannah's womb. Does that bother you?

Well, understand, if you will, that life was much different in Hannah's day than it is in ours. That is quite obvious. But the understanding of God's way of doing things was also vastly different. It really shouldn't surprise us that Hannah's situation would be interpreted in this manner. God was seen as more hands-on in those days. Life was more cause and effect. That which we know to be the acts of nature, in the days of the Hebrew judges, were attributed to God. But then again, they also thought the world was flat. Who knows what they believed when it came to the sun and moon and stars! Yet, we can also learn from this kind of story that God chose then and chooses now to work the divine purpose and will in our lives on God's terms and as the Lord wants to do so. Just exactly how that occurs cannot always be determined. We have to remain open to hearing a word from God that comes in a form we have not known before.

So, while we might be bothered by some of the interpretative aspects of this story, it can still teach us a great deal, if we will be open to it.

Hannah is reminded of her barrenness every day, no doubt, when she sees the children play; children who bear such a strong resemblance to their father, her beloved Elkanah, but look nothing at all like her because they were given birth by Peninnah, Elkanah's other—not to mention spiteful—wife. Her heart aches when she thinks she might never see her own children taken into the loving arms of their father and play with him. It is difficult for her to envision the day when her as-yet-unborn sons might be apprenticed into Elkanah's work. Hannah is barren. Hannah is incomplete. Hannah, like Naomi, is bitter.

And Peninnah, the other woman? Hannah will get no sympathy from her. In fact, Peninnah rubs it in at every opportunity. Hannah's emotional wounds are raw and bleeding and open for everyone to see, and Peninnah, with all the graceless vengeance she can muster, enjoys rubbing salt—alcohol even!—into those wounds. Life has become, if you will excuse yet another pun, in more ways than one, *unbearable* for poor Hannah.

"Hannah, why do you weep? Hannah, why do you not eat. Why is your heart sad? Am I not more to you than ten sons?" Elkanah tries to console his distraught wife, but it doesn't do any good. It is inevitable, if the normal course of things evolve, that Elkanah will precede his wife to the grave. Where will she be then? What will she do then? Without a son to comfort her and provide for her, she will be like Naomi who took for herself the name *Mara*. *Mara*, I will remind you, means *bitter*. Hannah will be left to the mercy of the merciless Peninnah. That's where she'll be. It will be hell on earth.

"Am I not more to you than ten sons?" Easy for him to say! He has children to bounce on his knee. He has children with whom he can do baby talk, play hide-and-seek, watch grow into maturity. Hannah has no children, for she is barren. "Barren" is one of those words that conveys so perfectly what it represents that no definition is necessary. Hannah's life has become barren in more ways than one, but there is only one solution to her problem. Hannah needs a son.

She decides to take her problem directly to God. Again we encounter one of those phrases in scripture which, if we just pass by it and read it at face value, will lose much of its meaning. Hannah addresses God as "Lord of hosts." It is the title usually reserved by the Israelites for addressing God as the One who fights for Israel against oppression.[1] It is used when the person praying is considering God in military terms. It is a clue that Hannah considers herself to be the one who is oppressed.

In addition to barrenness, desperation is a recurring theme in the scriptures. In her desperation, Hannah makes her deal with God. If the Lord will look upon her misery and take pity upon her, if the God of Israel whose mighty works are well known in the faith community, will respond to her

1. Michael E. Williams, editor, *Storyteller's Companion to the Bible: Old Testament Women*, Vol. 4 (Nashville: Abingdon Press, 1993), p. 119.

need and give her a male child, she will do something in return that is really quite extraordinary. She will attach a Nazarite vow to her son, from the moment he is born until the day he dies. He will drink no wine and never put a razor to his hair. He will be given, consecrated, to the Lord.

The average Nazarite vow lasted only thirty days. Hannah's son, if God so chose to grant her desire, would live all his days with this commitment. What an extraordinary promise, not only for herself but also for her son! This is another part of the story that may trouble us. How can she make a promise for her son that will commit him to a vow for all his life that he might not want to fulfill?

When Eli, the temple priest, is finally convinced that Hannah isn't drunk but is moving her lips in prayer, he grants to Hannah the bargain she has put before God. "Go in peace; the God of Israel grant the petition you have made to him." Was it a priestly blessing or a promise? Did Eli have the power to answer for God? Did he know something she didn't know? Was he just trying to get this troublesome woman out of the temple, or was it merely wishful thinking on his part?

We don't have an answer to these questions, we only know that God did have mercy on this servant Hannah and gave her what she asked for: a son. And then, when her son Samuel is weaned, she fulfills her part of the vow she made before God. She takes him to Eli, the priest who had given her his blessing, and she gives her son to him! All those years of barrenness, all those tears, all those times of anticipating her heart's desire, and God finally hears her desperate cry and grants her wish. And what does she do? She gives her beloved son to an old priest who can't even keep his own sons under control. Life can indeed be strange sometimes, can't it? Does she anticipate, now that her womb is opened, that she will bear other children to replace the one she is giving up? Is the first child simply a test case? Does she give Samuel to the Lord as an offering, something like a tithe, except in this case we're not talking about barley or sheep or money but a child?

What a tremendous sacrifice! Yet, to be honest, Hannah's story is included in the Old Testament because she is the mother of an important man, her firstborn son Samuel, who directs his nation in that short period of time when the leadership of Israel moves from the judges to the kings. However, she could have been the mother of a nameless nobody, and her story would still be quite compelling. What a strange story it is but also what a tremendous sacrifice it depicts!

Let us admit that we don't know much about sacrifice. And quite frankly, it is our tendency to associate it with a negative experience. We think that sacrifice is wrapped up in self-denial, in giving up something we covet. Maybe that is why we aren't a sacrificial people. We don't like to give up things that are near and dear to our hearts.

But a recent insight has come my way, and I want to share it with you. In the Old Testament, a sacrifice was not necessarily self-denial; it was an act of consecration, of giving. The person who gave the sacrifice to God wanted to make sure it was the best he could possibly give. Then, once given, it was up to God as to whether the sacrifice would be blessed, would become sacred.[2]

What do we generally think of when we consider the issue of sacrifice? Time, money, possessions? I know of one church that was promoting a financial campaign and urged

2. Mary Zimmer, *Sister Images* (Nashville: Abingdon Press, 1993), p. 70.

its members to give up items that were precious to them. One woman laid her wedding ring on the altar, much to the amazement and unhappiness of her husband who had given it to her! Is that real sacrifice, or is it manipulation? The word *sacrifice* can be threatening to us, for good reason!

Hannah doesn't seem to help. Her sacrifice appears to be so radical, so off the wall, that, even though it might make for a good story, it doesn't have much relevance for us. Think of all she will miss by not being able to watch her child grow and mature. Her influence and motherly affection will never be known by her son, a son she wanted and yearned for for so many years. Today we don't think very highly of people who give their children away, do we?

But try to put yourself in her place. Is it not true that having a child and giving him to the service of God is better than not having a child at all? There aren't any guarantees of course, but what if her child grows up to become a leader of his people? What if the very destiny of Israel is changed for the good because of her son? What if? What if?

Hannah was willing to trust God with the "what if." And because of that, God chose to make sacred her sacrifice. God took what she was willing to give, her son, and bless her sacrifice many, many times over.

Are you and I willing to trust God with the "what if" of our lives? Are we willing to give the Lord that, which in return, will be made sacred? The first and finest gift, of course, is the gift of ourselves. To do that, is to give God our future, our "what if," trusting that God will take what we are yet to be, where we are yet to go, what we are yet to give, and bless it, making it sacred in the Lord's sight.

I would encourage you to consider where you are going in your life. Having dreams, setting goals, making plans . . . all of that is good. I do it myself. But somewhere in the midst of all that is the unknown, the "what if," the unplanned and undreamed of our lives. Give it to God, and the Lord will take that which is now barren and make it rich and good. God will take your sacrifice and make it sacred. And God will bless you as God blessed our sister Hannah.

new testament

MARY,
THE MOTHER OF JESUS
"more than a mother can take"

My soul magnifies the Lord, and my spirit rejoices in God my Savior, for he has looked with favor on the lowliness of his servant (Luke 1:46).

When we lived in Nashville, Tennessee there was constant talk about the huge mall that was going to be built in our community. It would be the largest mall in Tennessee! How excited we were! You see, in those days, if you wanted to go "malling," you had to traverse the busy streets of west Nashville to make your way to Green Hills or 100 Oaks. It would generally take twenty to thirty minutes, depending on the time of day and the traffic load.

There was a great deal of anticipation at first in regard to the mall that was yet to come . . . and yet to come . . . and yet to come. Finally, we all agreed: it was probably just a lot of talk. After a while, everyone simply dismissed it as idle gossip.

I wonder if that was something of how it was in the days of Mary and Joseph. There had once been so much talk of the

Coming One, the Messiah, and now, well, not much stock was put in the idle talk anymore. In fact, it had become a mantra that many a Jew would use in order to get out of an obligation, or just as an all-purpose excuse for a lot of things. "When the Messiah comes . . ."

"I will repay you the loan I owe you, when the Messiah comes."

"You will get an increase in pay, when the Messiah comes."

"I will do this, I will do that, when the Messiah comes."

Today, we may say something like, "Oh yeah, that'll happen all right; when it's a cold day in July!"

Same thing. "When the Messiah comes . . ." It was a pretty safe bet the Messiah wasn't going to come.

You know how it is. The same thing is true with the second coming of Christ. In every generation, during the last two thousand years, there have been those who fervently looked for the return of Christ. Some have even sold their homes, quit their jobs, and camped out on the very spot where they think Jesus will return. Others write books about it, predict how and when and where, and often become quite wealthy off the gullibility and poor biblical understanding of others. However, we must admit that the Apostle Paul believed in the soon return of Christ and had to deal with the repercussions of its not coming to fruition during his lifetime. But most of us are content to let God determine when it will be—which, of course, is what Jesus said we should do. That attitude is made easier, especially after the fervor of the millennium frenzy. We tend not to put much stock in it, though that response may be just as unbiblical as trying to force it upon our calendars.

Surely, the same dynamic existed in the days when Augustus was emperor of the Roman Empire and Quirinius was governor of Syria. In the minds of most, there was just too much talk about the Messiah and not enough action. And then one day an angel appears to a young maiden in Nazareth, and the world since that time has never been the same.

Having been given the angel's promise, the young maiden Mary offers to God the prayer known as the *Magnificat.* Gabriel's message, of course, is that Mary is highly favored of God and would give birth to his own unique son. Luke tells us she was greatly troubled by his message. A milder interpretation is that she was *perplexed.*

Perplexed? I'd say so. Even in a day in which such extraordinary things seemed to have occurred more readily than in ours, you just didn't have an angel come knocking on your door on a frequent basis. Mary may have been only perplexed. I would have been apoplectic! However, if "greatly troubled" conveys it best, what Mary doesn't know is, this is just the beginning. She ain't seen nothin' yet! "Greatly troubled" doesn't even begin to cover it.

When Mary says, "Here am I, the servant of the Lord; let it be to me according to your word," do you think she had a clue as to what she was getting into? Doubtful, isn't it? But did she really have a choice? Would *you* have turned down an angel?

A better question, perhaps, is this: Do you think that, years later, standing at the foot of the cross, if Mary had it to do all over again, she would say, "Let it to be me according to your word"? Or do you think she would have offered the first-century equivalent of, "Well, if it's all right with you, I think I'll pass. You see, I have a more mundane existence in mind"?

We have seen, during our previous excursion through the lives of women depicted in the Old Testament, that a dominant thread in the stories of these women is barrenness and the desperation that accompanies it. Mary has just visited with her cousin Elizabeth who is also with child. Elizabeth's story continues the theme of older women, childless for many years, conceiving through the direct intervention of God.

But not with Mary. What a departure her story takes! From the issue of childlessness, and its cultural ramifications in Old Testament times, to that of an out-of-wedlock conception! Talk about a one-eighty! We've definitely changed course with Mary's story. From Sarah and Rebekah and Hannah, who so desperately wanted male children, to this fresh flower of a young maiden for whom that is the furthest thing from her mind. It's almost as if God decides that with the coming of his Son, and all the changes that will occur as a result, it's time to change his method of operations as well. Perhaps it is God's way of saying, "Behold, I do a new thing!"

Though she and all the other women had always been forced to sit apart from the men in worship at the synagogue, Mary still knows the desire that burns in the heart of every devout Jew. It is the coming of the Anointed One, the Chosen, the Messiah. Could it be possible that He is about to come? And what is this? She is to be the instrument of the Lord through whom the Anointed One will come? Can it really be true?

Responding to that which is yet to come about, especially when it is announced by an angel, always involves risk.

Yet there is one thing that is still definitely known, of which there is no question. Mary isn't married—not yet. She is betrothed or engaged, but not married. Gabriel is telling her it's a done deal. She has conceived without knowing Joseph or any other man. Gabriel has told her this conception is of the Holy Spirit. "For nothing is impossible with God," Gabriel says. "Nothing is impossible with God."

Yeah, right. Tell that to the early morning busybodies down at the village well. Tell that to the local rabbi who looks rather suspiciously at anybody who doesn't rise to the level of his spirituality. Tell that to her family, to Joseph's family. It will mean disgrace! No wonder Joseph took her to Bethlehem for the census. It was a great excuse to get out of town and away from all the wagging, clucking, self-righteous tongues.

How old do you think Mary may have been? Fourteen, fifteen? Adulthood, especially for women, began much earlier in those days than in ours. Do you think Mary's response was really as quick, and as certain, as Luke portrays it to have been? Or did Luke, for the sake of space, give us the *Reader's Digest* condensed version of the conversation between Mary and Gabriel? Perhaps Gabriel said something like, "Mary, sit down. Let's talk. This is going to take awhile." And then he launches into this long soliloquy, explaining what it was going to be like for her. After hearing all the angel has to say, about the nature of Jesus' life, how he will be different from all the other children—even her own—how he will have to strike out on his own and do what his heavenly Father called upon him to do . . . after hearing all this, taking it in, letting it turn over and over in her mind and heart, did she then say to him, "Let it be to me according to your word"? Do you think that is how it might have been?

I don't know. I don't know. But I suspect that Gabriel could have stayed there a month and not been able to prepare Mary for what she would experience over the next three decades or so.

What we know about the childhood of Jesus is not even enough to be defined as sketchy. We do know about the temple incident when he was twelve. Unknowingly left behind by his family after the celebration of Passover, Mary and Joseph return to Jerusalem to search for him. They find him in the temple. When they question him as to why he had not left the Holy City with their family, his response is, *Did you not know that I must be about my Father's business*?

It makes you wonder about some things, doesn't it? Did Mary ever lift a hand to Jesus when she disapproved of his behavior? Did she ever disapprove? Did he misbehave or was he perfect even as a child? If so, what kind of questions would that leave in Mary's mind? After all, how would you like to have raised a perfect child? We all know that our children are not perfect. Our grandchildren are, but not our children. Mary gave birth to him, but was he really hers, or did his demeanor always leave her with the impression that his allegiance was given to Someone Else?

By the time Jesus was about thirty and was beginning his public ministry, the story and what his mission is that she encourages him to take care of the problem which occurs.

The host has run out of wine. She simply turns to her eldest child and says, "They have no wine."

That could have been a simple statement; it certainly seems innocent enough. Or it could mean that she thought it his duty, as the eldest, to run down to the convenience market and buy some wine to save the host the public embarrassment. Or, it could have been her way of letting Jesus know she thought it was about time for him to reveal his nature, even if he didn't.

That seems just like what a Jewish mama would do, and as my friend John Killinger once put it in an Advent sermon, "Everybody ought to have a Jewish mama." But we know how Jesus took it. He thought she was telling him how to do his business, and his response is rather harsh. *Woman*—notice he doesn't even call her "Mama"—*Woman, what concern is that to you or to me? My hour is not yet come.*

In telling us this story, John doesn't give us Mary's reaction; just her words. She turns to the servants of the house and says, with rather tight lips, I would imagine, "Do whatever he tells you." There's a very interesting subtlety here. Jesus may have been short to his mother with his curt reply, and Mary may not have appreciated her son's tone of voice, she still knew what he would do. She was his mama. She knew he would take care of the situation. "Do whatever he tells you."

And then there's Capernaum. Jesus's public popularity is at its all-time high. The crowds can't get enough of him, his teachings and his miracles. However, word has obviously filtered down to Nazareth that the behavior Jesus has been exhibiting lately is rather strange. So Mary decides to find out for herself what is going on. She gathers up all of Jesus' siblings (obviously, father Joseph is now dead) and they head for the seashore village of Capernaum. Jesus, as usual, is surrounded by people, and messengers come to tell him his family wants to see him. Are you familiar with his response? *Who are my mother and my brothers*? He points to those who are sitting around him. *Here are my mother and my brothers! Whoever does the will of God is my brother and sister and mother.*

Ouch. It's not fair, is it? He was hers. Had he not come from her loins?! Yet, instinctively she knew he was not hers. It was as if he belonged to a higher allegiance. *Who are my mother and my brothers*?

Did Gabriel tell her it would be like this? Look at what we are told the angel did say. He talked about how great her child would be, how he would be the Son of God. The Lord would give him his throne and his kingdom would have no end. He would be holy! Gabriel never said a word about his turning his back on his mama. On second thought, Gabriel conveniently left out a number of things. It was like signing a contract with microscopic print. Mary never read the small print. She couldn't. Gabriel held the contract in his hand throughout the entire conversation, with his thumb obscuring the difficult parts. The only time Mary touched it was when she signed on the dotted line.

But the worst, of course, the absolute worst, was the cross. Standing at the foot of the cross, as she thought back over all the things that had happened between herself and her eldest son, as she remembered the strange things he said and the odd things he did—as her heart was breaking—do you think she was tempted to say to God (Gabriel, are you listening in to this prayer as well?), "This is more than a mother can take"?

She had become accustomed somewhat to this strange way of living, always dealing with the unknown, never knowing what Jesus would say or do next. She always, when it came to her son Jesus (she didn't even get to choose his name!), had to struggle with the unknown, the mysterious.

When Jesus openly, finally, tells his disciples what will happen in Jerusalem—that he will undergo great suffering, be rejected by the religious establishment, be killed, and after three days rise again—is Mary there? Does she hear his words along with the disciples? Does she pass it off like the others, or does she take it to her brooding heart and say to herself, "This is more than a mother can take"?

Perhaps those thoughts, those words, crossed her mind and lips. But I would encourage you to look fully into the face of Mary, the mother of Jesus, and see that in the midst of the pain and suffering and agony that comes with such a terrible tragedy as losing one's son—especially like *this*—Mary never backed down from the commitment she had made years ago to a certain angel named Gabriel. Never. And she wasn't going to do it now, not even in the face of the cross. "Let it be to me according to your word."

Usually, our image of Mary is that of the adoring mother, bending over the manger, peering into the red and wrinkled face of her newborn son. I would like to suggest a different image for Mary, at least for this day. Look into her face as she stares at the dying form of her son, and see the steely determination, the rock hard resolve, the earnest commitment. God had asked a great deal of Mary. There may have been those times when she thought it was more than she could take, but not once, not once, did she back down from her commitment to her God.

Can we say the same? In the face of life's difficulties,

whatever they may be, are we found saying, "Let it be to me according to your word"? When things don't go our way, and we think it is more than we can take, do we pray, "Let it be to me according to your word"?

Perhaps now is the time for us to look deeply within our hearts to determine the true level of our faith and commitment to God. And if there is something lacking, and we cannot honestly echo Mary's words, this may be the moment for us to ask God's grace to give us the resolve necessary to do his will at all costs. We may be tempted to think that life gives us more than we can take, but if we will have within ourselves the same resolve as Mary, the rest of our life's journey may just be the best part of the adventure.

MARY OF BETHANY

"THE BETTER PART"

There is need of only one thing. Mary has chosen the better part, which will not be taken away from her (Luke 10:42).

While a seminary student, I pastored a small rural church about fifteen miles west of Lawrenceburg, Kentucky. The name of the church was *Friendship*, and, indeed, that is the most singular thing those good folk gave us in the almost three years we were with them. They provided us with wonderful friendship. And for that, we will always be grateful.

It was what was called a "Sunday-only" church. That meant we would drive out on Sunday morning, spend the day on "the church field," and after Sunday evening worship head back west to our home in Louisville. A different family would host us each week for lunch. Lunch? Did I say lunch? It wasn't just lunch, it was always a *feast*! Three or four choices of meat, garden fresh vegetables that would make your salivary glands work overtime, topped off with pies and cakes and all manner of lush and creamy desserts. Washed down with succulent, cold iced tea, it was a veritable cornucopia of all things worth eating. It makes my palate salivate just to think of it still. I can assure you I weighed more when I left the church than when I first started.

My wife and I noticed something else as well. You couldn't help but see it. The hostess hardly ever sat down to eat. And when she did, it was usually at a separate table. You see, having the preacher over generally meant that extended family or other friends were invited as well, so the table would be crowded. The very one who prepared and served the sumptuous meal rarely enjoyed it at the same table as her guests. She usually ate later, after everyone else was satisfied.

We would often protest, asking her to join us, but to no avail. It was the lay of the land, the culture operative in that part of the world. That's just the way it was done "in those parts."

I am reminded of those long ago rural Kentucky scenes every time I read about the household of Lazarus, Mary, and Martha. There are two sisters and a brother who live together in the village of Bethany, not far from Jerusalem. No mention is made of other siblings or parents. We are not told why or how, but we do know they were the close friends of Jesus.

One day Jesus is their honored guest. Presumably, he has the disciples with him, so quite a crowd has descended upon their home. While Jesus is in the living room telling the others about the kingdom of heaven, Martha is slaving away in the kitchen. Pots and pans are everywhere, breads and pastries are baking in the oven, the tea is brewing and the only thing that is becoming overcooked is Martha's temper.

"Mary, Mary, I need you to . . . Mary, where are you?

Has she wandered off again? I tell you, I can't ever count on that girl to do anything right. Just when I need her most she's off again. Usually she's out by the olive tree daydreaming. I need her help, and as usual, she's nowhere to be found. She's about as useless as a parasol in a whirlwind. Mary! Mary! Where are you?"

Have you ever wondered who was the older of the two sisters? It would be just like an older sister to command the kitchen, wouldn't it? After all, firstborns are usually the go-getters in every family. So, it could easily be conjectured that Martha was older, maybe even the oldest in the family. And Luke refers to it as Martha's home. However, if she were older, don't you think she would have had the authority, that comes with age, to confront Mary herself about what she perceives as her little sister's laziness? Rather than going to Jesus, in an effort to get him to intervene on her behalf, you would think she would simply take matters into her own hands. I guarantee you that is what my older brothers would have done.

It's interesting, isn't it? She doesn't say anything to Mary, but does take issue with Jesus. Maybe it's his fault. "Do you not care that my sister has left me to do all the work by myself? Tell her then to help me." Ah . . . Maybe Martha isn't the older of the two after all. Perhaps, instead, she is Jesus's elder, so she goes to him. She certainly doesn't mind bossing him around, does she? "Tell her to help me."

Or, perhaps, she speaks to Jesus out of great respect. She does, after all, refer to him as "Lord." Maybe she looks upon him as something of a parental figure and asks him to intervene, just as a child will try to gain the support of a mother or father when a sibling is misbehaving. "Mom, she pulled my hair!" "Dad, he looked cross-eyed at me!"

It is true that Martha doesn't come across looking very good in this story, at least from Jesus' perspective. Mary is praised and Martha is left holding the bag; or, at least the casserole pan. *Martha, Martha, you are worried and distracted by many things; there is need of only one thing.* ***Mary has chosen the better part****, which will not be taken away from her.*

Most of us are pretty familiar with this story, aren't we? From our days in Sunday School, it has always been one of the favorites of children. I'm not sure why, but it's simply one of those accounts in the New Testament that you tend to remember. My guess, however, is that it is hard for us to believe Mary did the right thing. After all, Martha comes off as looking helpful and industrious. The Greek word used to describe her work in the kitchen is *diakonia*, from which we get the word *deacon*. She is in the worthy role of a servant, and Jesus chides her for it! On the other hand, Mary appears to be lazy. We generally don't cotton very well to lazy people, and for that reason we are left rather perplexed about this "better part" Jesus is talking about. When it came to Sunday dinner in Kentucky, my appreciation would have been much higher for Martha than Mary.

My guess is that those of us who grew up with this story have often wondered what was so great about what Mary did. After all, she merely sat and listened. Martha is the one who slaves away in the kitchen. Martha is the one with the work ethic. Martha is the one who wants everything to be just right for her special guest. All Mary did was shirk her womanly duties, sit at Jesus's feet, and soak in his stories about the kingdom. Here she is, lazy as can be, and Jesus gives her the credit for it! It doesn't seem fair, does it?

So, how do we reconcile what Jesus says with our feelings about the people in this story? We might just find some insight in a couple of clues Luke gives us. First of all, he doesn't tell us directly that the village is Bethany. We know it is Bethany from the two stories John provides in his gospel. Luke refers to it as "a certain village," and we can pretty well guess that he has a reason for doing so. The other clue is where he places the story. It follows hard on the heels of Jesus's parable of the Good Samaritan.

Let's consider the clues. Why doesn't Luke go ahead and tell us the "certain" village is Bethany? After all, he is usually quite detailed in his writings when it comes to his travelogues. Just look at the other New Testament book he wrote, The Acts of the Apostles, and you will see that. Bethany is just outside Jerusalem, about two miles, and if you look carefully at the way Luke tells of Jesus's journeys during this particular time, you will know that while it is true Jesus is on his way to Jerusalem (Luke has already said he has "set his face" to the Holy City), Bethany isn't even close to where he was just before and where he will be after this story is completed. In other words, this encounter likely occurred at a different time, but Luke has placed his story here for a specific purpose, after the parable of the Good Samaritan. Why? What's his point? I'm glad you asked.

Luke isn't just telling a story, he is offering an interpretation. Luke is telling us that in being so anxious to serve dinner for her Master and Friend, Martha is much like the priest and the Levite who passed by the man left by the side of the road to die. In her busyness, she has not allowed time for the most important considerations of life. But, her sister Mary has. Mary has found "the better part."

"Mary," as John Killinger puts it, "has the soul of the Samaritan."[1] Of far greater concern to her is the opportunity to learn from Jesus, and in her learning she is expressing her love for him. It is in John's Gospel that she is identified as the one who, in front of everyone, anoints Jesus' head with expensive ointment. John's story, with a different twist, may very well be taken from the same account we find in Luke's Gospel. "The better part," to which Jesus refers, is Mary's complete devotion to him and to his kingdom. Anything else, Jesus is saying, is less, and in the eternal scheme of things, while perhaps important, is secondary to seeking Christ and his purpose. So Jesus praises Mary for seeking "the better part."

But ask the Jewish rabbis if her behavior is appropriate. Listen to the writing of a certain rabbi from Jerusalem who lived about 150 years before Christ. "He that talks much with womankind brings evil upon himself and neglects the study of the Law and at the last will inherit Gehenna."[2] Another Jewish writer is quoted as saying, "Let thy house be a meetinghouse for the Sages and sit amid the dust of their feet and drink in their words with thirst . . . (but) talk not much with womankind."[3]

So you see, this story really is amazing. It reveals Jesus and Mary openly breaking the social and religious code of their day, and shows Jesus's willingness to let Mary be who and what she chooses to be.

1. John Killinger, *The Gospel of Contagious Joy* (Waco: Word Books, 1980), p. 69.

2. Evelyn and Frank Stagg, *Woman in the World of Jesus* (Philadelphia: The Westminster Press, 1978), p. 52.

3. Leander E. Keck, Editor, *The New Interpreter's Bible* (Nashville: Abingdon Press, 1995), Vol. IX, p. 231.

Jesus also gives Martha the freedom to be Martha. He doesn't go into the kitchen and drag her out to join everyone. He lets her stay in the kitchen if that is where she wants to be. He simply lets her know that her choice is not the same, and frankly, is not as worthy as that of her sister. Jesus let Martha be Martha. That is not surprising. But he also let Mary be Mary, and that is surprising because it flies in the face of the accepted custom in that day.

"Lord, do you not care that my sister has left me to do all the work by myself? Tell her then to help me."

Martha, Martha . . . Martha, Martha, Martha, Martha. . . . That's just about the only way it can be interpreted. By repeating her name, Jesus is offering her a mild rebuke. *Martha, Martha . . .* Jesus is lamenting her behavior. Her name cannot be called twice without our knowing that what will follow is Jesus's correction of her attitude. It is Jesus's way of telling her she has got the cart before the horse. The problem is, she has been told all her life that the cart belongs before the horse! Somehow, Mary has gotten the correct message. Why? How?

Because she is young? Perhaps. But there may just be a different reason. Mary, while the blood kin of Martha, is cut from a different piece of cloth. She has a different longing, a different perspective. She longs for something other than endless dirty dishes. She has a spirit about her, a hunger and thirst that attracts her to Jesus, and he to her. She knows there are things in life more important than the obvious. She has a craving for God's kingdom to be present in her. She has a longing for the eternal.

Do we?

It is not a stretch to suggest that Luke's story about Mary reveals in Jesus the willingness to recognize the right of every person, male or female, to follow the dictates of conscience and of the heart. He defends Mary's privilege of being who and what she chooses, not merely falling lock-step into the narrow confines prescribed for women in her day. Mary is the primary example of how Jesus has liberated us all to fulfill what we consider God's purpose for us on this earth.

And what she has—"the better part"—*will not be taken away from her.*

There is need of only one thing, Jesus tells Martha, and Mary has found it. It is the hearing of what Jesus has to say in regard to the kingdom. What Mary has chosen *will not be taken away from her.* The meal will literally pass, but the hearing of the word will continue to bless and guide, nourish and sustain. *Blessed are those who hunger and thirst after righteousness,* Jesus says, *for they shall be filled.*

Does this mean that what Martha is doing has no value? I hope not. I enjoy a well-prepared meal as much as anyone, and remember with great appreciation and affection the efforts put forth by those wonderful ladies in Kentucky. They helped to nourish and sustain their pastor! Jesus often used allusions to meals and went to great effort to provide physical sustenance for the multitudes on more than one occasion. But, even then, the food itself was secondary to a larger and higher purpose. The fish and the bread, of themselves, were symbolic of the presence of the kingdom. Jesus didn't just want the people to have full bellies, he wanted their hearts, their souls, to be filled with the presence and power afforded by his heavenly Father's kingdom. *That* is the better part.

Let us also not forget that Jesus was accused by his enemies of being a glutton and a drunkard. Why? Because he was caught in the act of overeating and being drunk? Of course not. Their accusations had nothing to do with the volume of his intake. They had everything to do with those who shared his table—the sinners. Why did Jesus have fellowship with known sinners? So he could introduce them to "the better part," the kingdom. He obviously found in them a more eager audience than those who chose to shut themselves out of the kingdom.

Jesus spent time with people who were marginalized by the their society, placed in a less than favorable slot or position by the social code of the day. The Samaritan, in Jesus's story just prior to this passage, fits that category because of his race. Mary of Bethany had less than full privileges because of her gender. And both, Jesus is pointing out, are wonderful candidates for discipleship.

That is Jesus's way. Jesus comes to those who wonder what their value might be to God and the kingdom and says, *Follow me.* Jesus comes to those who question whether they have what it takes to be counted as worthy of God's grace and attention, and says, *Well done, my good and faithful servant.* Jesus comes to those who, by all outward appearances, couldn't possibly have their names written in the Book of Life, and says, *Come, O blessed of my Father, inherit the kingdom prepared for you.* And Jesus comes to the religiously smug and comfortable and complacent and cocky and says, *Depart from me, for I never knew you.*

Beware the feeling that you fit all the necessary spiritual criterion while you look down your nose at those who do not appear to be as worthy as yourself. They may just be the very ones who have chosen the better part.

This story of the sisters of Bethany tends to keep us off guard, doesn't it? That just may be for our good. If nothing else, may it serve notice to us that we dare not think we have it made when it comes to the kingdom. If this story keeps us on our spiritual toes, so be it. Perhaps it will keep us searching for the better part.

MARTHA

"True Believer"

Yes, Lord, I believe that you are the Christ, the Son of God, the one coming into the world (John 11:27).

We had not been home long from a Friday night high school basketball game when the telephone rang. The news was not good. A young woman in our congregation had died earlier that day, shot by the estranged husband of a friend. She had taken her friend to his home, but while she was still sitting in the car he took out a long-range hunting rifle and shot her through the windshield. She did not actively attend our church, but her mother was a devoted member. When I arrived at the home, the grief and shock of such a loss was, needless to say, quite profound.

I had experienced before the grief that arises from a senseless death, but it was reinforced for me all over again. Grief, of itself, is bad enough. But when grief has frustration and perplexity and questioning added to the mix, it is that much harder to accept. For example, when a teenager commits suicide; when a person overdoses on drugs; when a murder, such as one like this, is committed randomly; when people go crazy and shoot up businesses and day care centers; grief is intensified in such circumstances.

The mother of the young woman who was murdered felt this kind of frustration. Added to her grief was the manner in which her daughter died and the suspicion, later corroborated, that drug use was involved. Sometimes, as this mother could tell you, there are several layers to grief, emotions that become companions to grief and make it that much harder to take.

Such was true of Martha of Bethany. John's account portrays both Martha and her sister Mary to be consistent with the behavior they exhibited in the story we considered in the last chapter from Luke's Gospel. Martha, purveyor of pots and pans and custodian of the family kitchen, Martha the active one, rushes out to meet Jesus when she hears he is coming into the village. Mary, the contemplative one, whose preference is to sit at Jesus's feet and listen to him weave his stories of the kingdom, stays home.

Martha leaves the crowd of mourners and goes to the edge of town to meet Jesus. She is not concerned anymore about the preparation of food. Eating is largely forgotten when one is in grief. Besides, everyone knows that on the occasion of death, others bring food to the house. It is a wonderful thing to do, but I've often wondered if the greater gift would not be to come in after the meal is completed and clean up. With all of the mourners who have come to Bethany from Jerusalem, Martha has all the kitchen help she needs. Now, she needs to talk to her friend Jesus.

Still acting like a big sister, however, she quietly reproaches Jesus for his tardiness. "Lord, if you had been here, my brother would not have died." In fact, she "sounds bitter and exhausted."* Same old Martha. She seems to be happiest when she's complaining about something.

Sometimes people make a statement and you know instinctively that what they are saying involves some hidden meaning. There is a personal agenda to what they are saying. That must be true here. I believe there's a lot of "stuff" in Martha's statement, and we shouldn't take it simply at face value. She is not exactly telling Jesus something he doesn't already know.

"Lord, if you had been here, my brother would not have died."

Martha is implying something very important to her. Jesus has let her down. Earlier in this narrative we are told that while their brother Lazarus was still ill, the sisters had sent a message to Jesus for him to come immediately. He didn't. In fact, he stayed where he was for several days, and he did it intentionally. It seemed so out of character that his disciples questioned him about it.

Jesus has made what appears to be a huge emotional withdrawal from Martha and Mary. Stephen Covey uses this kind of language in his book, *First Things First*, but the concept surely has its origins in many places. The point is well-taken. In any relationship, for it to be healthy and strong, there have to be emotional deposits made on a regular basis. That way, when an occasional withdrawal is required, there is still enough strength in the relationship that it is not damaged. Jesus has made a huge emotional withdrawal with

*Mary Zimmer, *Sister Images* (Nashville, Tennessee: Abingdon Press, 1993), p. 76.

Martha. He has let her down, and she is not prepared to let him off the hook. The issue is too important for her to do that.

Martha seems to know the message she and her sister Mary had sent to Jesus was received by him, and, it was received in plenty of time for him to get to Lazarus before he died. She seems to sense that Jesus has taken his good old time in getting there. And she is right! She is grieving, and she is frustrated and perplexed and filled with questions—and perhaps not a little bit angry—all at the same time.

If that is true, her opening statement to Jesus may have actually been quite restrained. "Lord, if you had been here, my brother would not have died." She may have wanted to use stronger language than that! She evidently has discussed this very thing with Mary, for Mary repeats it later to Jesus when she sees him. In fact, she uses the exact same words. "Lord, if you had been here, my brother would not have died."

Yet, it's almost as if Martha is saying, "Now don't interrupt me. I need to get this off my chest. If you had been here, my brother would not have died. You are the only one in the world who could have helped him. Yet, you weren't here, and that has done nothing but add to our grief. Okay, okay . . . good, I'm glad that's over with. I feel better now." And then, as if all the frustration and anger are exorcized from her by that simple rebuke, she goes on to offer an amazing statement of faith: "But even now I know that God will give you whatever you ask of him."

She isn't just grieving. She is also disappointed and feeling that Jesus has let her down. Her grief has taken on added layers. But—and this is very important—it has not consumed her faith in Jesus.

After Luke's portrayal of Martha, we can be grateful that John's gospel offers us another picture of this woman. Frankly, if we were left only with Luke's version, we would probably find it difficult to muster up much affection or sympathy for her. But thanks to John, we are given an insight into her heart and soul that makes us grateful for her deep and abiding faith. If we only had the story in Luke, we might be tempted to think she was nothing but a sniveling, complaining workaholic. But thanks to John we know there is a lot more to her than that. Martha is really quite an extraordinary woman. "But even now I know that God will give you whatever you ask of him." What do you think she expected God to give Jesus? It's doubtful, frankly, that she had any real clue.

What follows is one of the most important exchanges between two people in all of scripture, if not the most important. *Your brother will rise again,* Jesus says. Note the tenderness in what he says. He does not say, "Lazarus will rise again," or "My friend will rise again." Taking great care to acknowledge the loving relationship between Martha and Lazarus, he says, *Your brother . . . Your brother will rise again.*

"I know . . ." Martha says, perhaps with resignation in her voice. "I know . . . I know that he will rise again . . ." Then, showing not only her deep piety but also her understanding of scripture, she says, "[I]n the resurrection at the last day." The Jewish belief in resurrection on a final day of judgment was, in the first century, a relatively late development, having begun in the age of the prophets. Martha is revealing that her biblical and theological understanding is quite good and up-to-date. "I know that he will rise again in the resurrection at the last day."

Like all good Jews, Martha believed there would eventually be a resurrection from the dead of all those who believe. She just didn't expect it to come so soon! She lets her Master and Friend know that she believes in the *concept* of resurrection, but Jesus quickly informs her that resurrection is not a concept, it is not merely a belief that is part of a faith system. It is not just a doctrine. *Resurrection is a person*! Resurrection is a relationship. Resurrection is Jesus Christ, and until we have an intimate relationship with him, we do not know, nor understand, resurrection.

Your brother will rise again, Jesus says.

"I know that he will rise again in the resurrection at the last day."

I, Jesus says to her, *I—I—I am the resurrection and the life; those who believe in me, though they die, yet shall they live, and whoever lives and believes in me shall never die.*

And then, as if not to let her off the hook, Jesus looks her in the eye and asks her directly, *Do you believe this*?

In his Gospel, John portrays Jesus uttering a number of what are called the "I AM" sayings. *I am the bread of life; I am the living water; I am the good shepherd.* It is here, right here, that Jesus reaches the climax of these "I AM" sayings. *I AM the resurrection and the life.*

But Jesus wants to be very specific with Martha in this powerful conversation. *Do you believe this*? he asks her. It seems to be very important to Jesus that she believe, almost as if her belief is a requirement before he can do anything about her tragic loss. "Martha, look me in the eye and tell me.

Do you believe this?" Can't you just see him taking her chin in his hand, forcing her to look him directly in the eye as he asks her this pivotal question? "Martha, my good and dear friend, Martha, *do you believe this?"*

There is a certain specificity to the gospel. It is important to know what others believe, yes. It is valuable to know what the church universal affirms doctrinally. In my particular church context, it is right and good to know what Baptists generally believe. But after all is said and done, we must come to that point when we can say clearly what it is *we* as individuals believe.

Do you believe this? Jesus asks Martha. *Do you believe this*?

Martha, do you believe that resurrection is not just a doctrine or belief? Or, as the crossword puzzles would answer, an "-ism"? Do you believe that resurrection is a person? "Martha, do you believe that *I* am the resurrection and the life?"

"Yes, Lord, I believe that you are the Christ, the Son of God, the One coming into the world." Martha's wonderful confession of faith is right up there with Simon Peter's, what church tradition has come to call "The Great Confession."

It is highly, highly significant that Martha expresses her true belief in Jesus *before* he raises her brother Lazarus from the dead. The resurrection of Lazarus does not create belief in Martha. She is already a true believer, which is more than you can say for a lot of the others. Actually, Jesus's miracle of bringing his friend from the grave is cause for just the opposite in many of the Jews who are there to witness it. They haven't come out to the hillside village of Bethany to mourn as much as they are there to spy. Nor are they there to confess their belief in Jesus. No sooner does Lazarus emerge from the grave than they run as fast as their legs will carry them to report to the Pharisees what has happened. From John's perspective, it is the final straw for the religious establishment. Now they know—they are without doubt—the Nazarene must die.

A question I've often wondered about is this: did Martha hesitate before she answered Jesus? John gives us no indication, but wouldn't it have been natural for her to do so? Did Jesus put her on the spot with his direct question? What if she had said no, she did not believe? Or, "Please, Lord, let me think about this a moment." Or, "Well, I want to, but I still have some lingering doubts." Or, "Well, frankly, you've let me down once. Who's to say you won't do it again?" But she didn't say anything like that, did she? She responded, evidently immediately, "Yes . . . Yes . . . Yes." "Yes, Lord, I believe." Martha was a true believer.

In fact, Martha's statement of faith ranks higher than that of any other in the Gospel of John. Look at the disciples. They are with Jesus every day. Yet, they wallow in their misunderstanding of the kingdom. Martha openly and honestly displays her faith *before* the miracle is done! She models for us all the response to Christ that is not dependent on a sign or some kind of evidence that corroborates Jesus's claims. In our consideration of Mary, Martha's sister, we made the point that Jesus allows Martha to be Martha. In this story, Martha accepts Jesus for who he is, not based merely on what he can do for her. Showing that she has not spent all her time in the kitchen, she says, "Yes, Lord, I believe that you are the Christ, the Son of God, the One coming into the world."

What tremendous faith Martha has! Even in the midst of her terrible grief, she is indeed a true believer.

In light of that, to what extent can Martha model for us true faith in Christ? Well, perhaps it is this: Each of us must come to that point when Jesus takes our chin in his hand and asks us directly and very specifically, "Do you believe? Do you believe that I am the resurrection and the life?" Has he ever done that to you? What was your response?

"Well, Lord, let me get back to you on that one."

"But this is kind of sudden. I'm not ready to respond."

"I tell you what . . . Let me get some things in order, clean up my house a bit, so to speak. Then we'll sit down and have a good, long chat about this."

"I'm afraid I'll have to give up something that means too much to me."

"I like my life as it is and I'm afraid you will want to change it."

"My friends, my family, my coworkers won't understand."

"Does this mean I'll have to be religious?"

Wouldn't you guess that by now Jesus has heard just about every excuse in the book? Do you really think you could offer an excuse, or a way out, that he hasn't already heard before millions and millions of times over?

Let Martha teach us this lesson, that when Jesus comes to us, looking us in the eye, taking our chin in his hand so we cannot possibly avoid him, asking, *Do you believe*? we have her courage and faith as we echo her words, "Yes, Lord, I believe." And may we do it without hesitation.

THE WOMAN AT THE WELL

"LIVING WATER"

If you knew the gift of God, and who it is that is saying to you, "Give me a drink," you would have asked him, and he would have given you living water (John 4:10).

Jesus, for the first time in John's gospel, is now on the move. He has called his disciples, performed his first miracle, and established a reputation (though admittedly, with the religious establishment it is not a good one). Now it is time to return to Galilee. In order to journey from Jerusalem to Galilee, he has to go through Samaria. In fact, that is the kind of language John uses. He says Jesus "*had* to go through Samaria."

Actually, he didn't. Most Jews successfully avoided traveling through this area because of their intense hatred of Samaritans. Better to avoid a fight than create one, and when a Jew traveled through Samaria it was like swimming in a lake; it was at his own risk. At the worst he could run into some real trouble. At the least, he would receive absolutely no hospitality whatsoever. You could go to the bank on that one.

This enmity between Jews and Samaritans had been going on for centuries, but by the time of this encounter between Jesus and the woman at the well of Sychar, it had been really intense for about two hundred years. It was just enough time for the hatred to have been drilled deeply into the psyche of every Jew and Samaritan.

A deacon in one of my previous churches told me one day that when traveling in the south he absolutely refused to go through Mississippi. He would take hours and travel hundreds of miles out of his way to avoid driving in Mississippi. Since that is my father's native state, his statement piqued my interest, so I asked him to explain. It seems he had once received a speeding ticket there and thought the whole thing was a scam. He had held a grudge against "The Magnolia State" ever since. I couldn't imagine what made him think it wasn't on the level, just because the "judge" held court in an old barn out in the middle of a field and would only take cash!

John says Jesus "*had* to go through Samaria." Well, if Jesus *had* to go through Samaria it was because he felt personally compelled to go through Samaria. He had a reason for doing it, a reason that fit his convictions and purpose. Awaiting him there was this most interesting encounter with the woman at the well of Sychar.

It is about noon and the sun is really starting to heat things up. While he is sitting there, presumably in the shade, a woman of the nearby village comes to draw water. This chance (?) encounter provides Jesus a perfect opportunity to quench his thirst. *Give me a drink,* he says to the woman, *Give me a drink.* On the surface, his request seems so direct, so demanding. No "please" or "would you mind?" Just, *Give me a drink.*

It makes me wonder if there wasn't an inflection in his voice that can't be captured in the written word. Did Jesus give it something of an Irish inflection? Have you ever noticed the Irish end all their sentences as if they are asking a question? Did it come across as, "Give me a drink?"? Probably not. Given the Middle Eastern culture of that day, and to a real extent even now, I suppose, interaction between people didn't allow for a great deal of subtlety.

Jesus is tired from his journey, and his request for a drink is the means by which he draws the woman into a deep theological conversation. Do not discount the idea that Jesus is indeed tired and thirsty from his journey. It could be he knew what would happen before the woman even arrived. But regardless, he is thirsty and uses their meeting as an opportunity to share with her the secrets of the kingdom.

Because of the cultural protocol of the day, which generally did not allow a man to speak to a woman in public (even his own wife!), it's doubtful the woman looked directly at Jesus when she replied, "How is it that you, a Jew, ask a drink of me, a woman of Samaria?"

John explains parenthetically that Jews did not share vessels with Samaritans or any other non-Jews. Why not? Well, like a parent sometimes does says to a child who is persistent in wanting to have something the parent doesn't want to give . . . just because. A Jew didn't drink from the same vessel as a Samaritan . . . just because. Period. End of discussion.

Actually, there was a reason and it wasn't because of health concerns. One of my sisters-in-law will not drink from the same glass as someone else, even her husband and children. She doesn't want to transfer her germs or pick up theirs. I understand this; well, sort of. Jews considered Samaritans non-Jews, though there was a strong blood kinship between the two peoples. But to drink from the same vessel as a non-Jew rendered a Jew unclean. The Jews were quite conscious of ritual purity. Again, it had nothing to do with hygiene. It was a religious, ritual thing.

Make no mistake about it. Jews would not drink from the same vessels as Samaritans. So you see what Jesus is doing here, don't you? Once again, he is breaking rules. He is a man talking publicly with a woman, and he is a Jew speaking to a Samaritan. And the discussion is theological in nature, a subject that is generally restricted to discussions among men. Women are not included in such talk. Jesus breaks rule after rule after rule with his unseemly and highly controversial behavior. The rules just don't mean anything to Jesus, especially if they separate people.

I've never been much of a Dodgers fan, when they were in Brooklyn or since their move almost fifty years ago to Los Angeles (Has it really been that long?). But I am a huge baseball fan, and that is why I know the following story.

The last Brooklyn Dodgers shortstop was a fellow from Louisville, Kentucky named Pee Wee Reese. I *was* a Pee Wee Reese fan. He was referred to as the "Southern Gentleman." In 1947, courtesy of Branch Rickey, the Dodgers' general manager, Reese was provided with a teammate whose skin color was different from his own. His new teammate's name was Jackie Robinson. On their way north from spring training in Florida to Brooklyn, the team stopped in Reese's hometown for a final exhibition game. When the starting lineup was announced, the crowd began screaming at Robinson. Many of the fans were hurling racial epithets at the Dodgers' second baseman. Without a word, Reese put his arm around the shoulders of his black teammate, and with that simple gesture the racial taunting ceased. The color of Robinson's skin didn't matter to Pee Wee Reese. The only thing that was of concern to him was whether the man knew how to play ball. And Jackie Robinson definitely knew how to play ball.

Underline this, write it in red if you must; it just doesn't matter to Jesus what the rules are, be they religious rules, social rules, or cultural rules. If they separate people, God's children, whether they are male or female, Jew or Gentile, rich or poor, religious or non-religious, Jesus disregards them. His behavior is determined by the kingdom of heaven, not some piddlin' kingdom on earth with its piddlin' rules. His role is to bring people together in the name of the One who has sent him to fulfill his mission. To Jesus, a person is a person, created in God's own image. Black or white, Jew or Gentile, male or female, such distinctions don't matter. It doesn't matter in Jerusalem or Galilee, and it doesn't matter here in Sychar in the heart of Samaritan territory. Jesus wants this nameless woman to fulfill God's intention for herself, and the only way she can do that is by knowing him, by partaking of "living water."

The water that I will give will become . . . a spring of water gushing up to eternal life. This is not a trickling stream to which Jesus refers. It is a constant flow, a veritable geyser of grace!

In her book, *Pilgrim at Tinker Creek*, Annie Dillard talks about ground water that feeds the earth. "Ground water seeps and slides," she says, "across and down, across and down, leaking from here to there minutely, at the rate of a mile a year." That's the kind of slow process that fed Jacob's well in Sychar. But in offering her living water, Jesus speaks of the well that is dug deep into the human heart. It is living water, not the kind that ". . . seeps and slides, across and down . . ." but that which gushes and flows freely.

If there is anyone in scripture who needed such a geyser of grace, it is the woman at the well. We are immediately given the clue that her life is not exactly orthodox. She comes to the well at noon. Women of that culture generally would draw their daily supply of water early in the morning while it was still cool. This woman comes in the heat of the day, evidently to avoid contact with the women of the village. Why? Because she is an outcast? Probably. We learn from her conversation with Jesus that she has had five husbands and is presently living with a man to whom she is not married. This woman could use some grace.

Imagine the impact such news would have had upon her. At first, she takes Jesus literally when he offers her water. What's he going to do, put a spigot in her house? No more coming to the well. Think of the time this would save her, not to mention the fact that she would no longer have to endure the heat or avoid the scornful looks and wagging tongues of the village women. Then, as the conversation continues, she slowly begins to realize that Jesus isn't speaking literally. What he is offering her is grace, pure and simple, and a lot of it! Living water, full-flowing grace, based not on anything she has to do but ask for it. Available to her, of all people. Of all people! Ostracized from her own people, she has been granted keys to the kingdom of heaven by this total stranger, a Jew at that! Living water indeed!

Some biblical commentators find it hard to believe that this woman, or any woman of that day, could have had five husbands, especially if divorce was involved. They suggest that her society just wouldn't have allowed such behavior. But perhaps her situation simply points out that of all the women in the village, the chances are quite good she is the most notorious. When it comes to her lifestyle and morality, she's definitely pushing the envelope!

The woman, at first, sees Jesus only in terms of the obvious. To her, he is a Jew. Nothing more, nothing less. It is not long, however, before she has to admit he must be a prophet. After all, he knows things about her he has no business knowing. Nevertheless, she is quite well versed in those issues that separate her people from people like Jesus. "Sir, I see that you are a prophet. Nevertheless, you are a Jew and our ideas of worship are not exactly on the same page."

Yes, says Jesus, *But the hour is coming, and is now here, when the true worshipers will worship the Father in spirit and truth, for the Father seeks such as these to worship him.* May I interpret? Jesus is telling this woman that in him people are not separated in their worship of God. We are all the same. The rules that apply on earth have no validity in the kingdom. In the kingdom, God makes the rules, and God is in the business of offering grace, not separation. She is talking about earthly realities. Jesus is sharing with her what is true in the kingdom of heaven, and the only way to participate in such a kingdom is to drink from the water that only he provides.

It is at this point in their conversation that the disciples return. They have been foraging in the village for food. When they arrive at the well, John tells us they didn't dare ask her, "What do you want?" And they weren't about to ask Jesus, "Why are you speaking with her?" But look into their eyes. They didn't have to say it. It is as clear as the nose on your face. They are puzzled by what has been going on at the well, and not a little bit bothered. Their quizzical looks give the woman the opportunity she needs to make her exit and return to the village to tell the people about this strange and wonderful man she has just encountered at the well. "Come and see a man who told me everything I have ever done! He cannot be the Christ, can he? Well, can he?"

Did you notice something in the way John tells this interesting story? When the Samaritan woman leaves Jesus and his disciples to return to the village, she leaves her water jar behind at the well. Why bother with well water when she can have that which leads to eternal life? The jar instantly becomes a symbol of her old life. She is so energized by this unexpected encounter with the Galilean Jew that she can't wait to run to the village and tell everyone what has happened to her.

Whenever a baptism is performed, in a sense, the baptismal candidates come to the waters of baptism carrying their water jars; jars that are symbols of their lives before accepting Christ as Lord and Savior. When they emerge from the water and walk out of the baptistry, they leave their jars behind.

But the Samaritan woman isn't the only one who gets a charge from this conversation. "Rabbi," the disciples say, "Eat something. Look, we have brought food from the village. You are tired and hungry. Eat something. We still have a long way to go to reach Galilee." But Jesus says to them, *I have food to eat that you do not know about.* "I have already been fed; fed by the opportunity to share the kingdom of grace with this woman in such dire need of what only I can give."

Jesus, as well as the woman, is charged by this encounter, energized by this conversation. To Jesus, this conversation with the woman symbolizes God's approval of what he is doing.

Once Jesus and the woman have been newly-charged by this fresh encounter of the Spirit, they must go their way, Jesus to Galilee where he will continue to perform his signs and proclaim the kingdom, the woman to the village people who know her so well, but who will no doubt be changed by that which has changed her.

In the previous chapter, John records Jesus' conversation with Nicodemus, the Jewish leader. He talks to Nicodemus about new birth. Here, he uses the symbol of living water. New birth, living water, it really doesn't matter what it is called. What does matter is that Nicodemus and the Samaritan woman see Jesus for who he is and what he has to give.

"He told me everything I have ever done," the woman tells her fellow villagers. Not said, but definitely implied, is that for her this is just the beginning of a new opportunity. To start over, to put the past behind her both emotionally and spiritually, to have her slate wiped clean. How wonderful that would be. She is forgiven! What a powerful word that is, *forgiven*! It is just the first trickle of grace that is to become living water, gushing forth into new life.

We all come to a time when we are invited to receive God's word of grace, to leave our jar at the well, and go tell what Christ has done for us. Is this your time? If so, drink from the water that never fails, and in it you will find the answer to your deepest needs. Come and drink of the living water that leads to eternal life.

THE WOMAN TAKEN IN ADULTERY

"Unmerited Forgiveness"

Let anyone among you who is without sin be the first to throw a stone at her (John 8:7).

Let's consider what may be for some a new word, shall we? The word for the day is *peripatetic.* You know it already? Good! Then let's do a refresher. **Peripatetic** (adj.) From the Greek. 1. of the philosophy or the followers of Aristotle, who walked about in the Lyceum while he was teaching. 2. moving from place to place; walking about; itinerant. (n.) a person who walks from place to place.*

The word for the day is *peripatetic.* It describes a person who is constantly on the go, and it illustrates perfectly Jesus's activities during this portion of his public ministry recorded in the Gospel of John. It is during the Feast of Booths and Jesus is moving in and out of Jerusalem, like a crafty boxer jabbing away at his opponent. He is here, here is there. The religious authorities would like to catch him, to nail him down (literally!), but he proves to be too elusive for them. John portrays for us, especially in the seventh and eighth

*David B. Guralnik and Joseph H. Friend, General Editors, *Webster's New World Dictionary of the American Language* (Cleveland & New York: The World Publishing Company, 1966), p. 1088.

chapters, the peripatetic Jesus.

It is important for us to know that Jesus has been skirmishing all week with the Pharisees, the scribes, and temple authorities. Because of the festival, the city is crowded with religious pilgrims, Jews who have come from everywhere to the Holy City to celebrate this important time of remembrance and devotion. It is an opportunity for the religious establishment to put on its best colors, and display its religion like a peacock spreads its tail feathers.

And Jesus, much to the chagrin of the Pharisees, with his teachings of the kingdom of heaven, is stealing the show. Could it go without saying that the religious leadership isn't too fond of Jesus at this present moment? It probably could, but let's say it anyway. The religious leadership isn't too fond of Jesus at this present moment.

According to John, some of the Jews were looking for him. He doesn't explain why. "Where is he?" they ask. "Where is he?" There is a great deal of anticipation involved in the Jewish religious feasts because it is a special time, but it is enhanced on this particular occasion because Jesus has brought a new and fresh perspective to everything. When he does show up, darting in and out of the temple like a gadfly, many of the Jewish pilgrims are clearly impressed by him personally and are astonished by his teachings. "How does this man have such learning," they ask, "when he has never taught?"

The Pharisees are trying to have Jesus killed, and when the temple police are unable to arrest him, they want to know why. "Never has anyone spoken like this!" the police officials say. They too are impressed! How in the world can they possibly arrest such a man, a man who obviously has such a deep and unique knowledge of God?!

The bottom line is, Jesus has turned Jerusalem on its collective ear. Everyone is abuzz over the Galilean.

So, the scribes and Pharisees try a different tack. They will trick Jesus into making a mistake, shaming him in front of the common folk who are so taken with him, and cause him to lose his popularity and credibility with the people. It may be a desperate strategy on their part, but it is the only strategy they have left.

They bring to Jesus a woman who has been taken in the "very act" of adultery. That, in itself, raises all kinds of questions. How did they find her? Did they know of her "lifestyle" before this incident with Jesus? Had they ignored it up to now, deciding to do something about it only when it would suit their purposes?

This narrative is generally referred to as "the woman taken in adultery." That is the way it is characterized in the title of this chapter because that is how we identify the story. It is familiar to most of us, and portions of it are rather publicly well-known, especially the statement by Jesus about casting stones. But the main emphasis isn't upon the woman. Not really. The real focus is upon this battle of wits between Jesus and the Pharisees. She is used by the Pharisees to discredit Jesus and trick him into making an error of judgment. The key phrase is that she "is being used by the Pharisees."

Though John gives us no indication of it, my guess is that at no time in scripture is Jesus more angry than he is at this particular time. He reserved his greatest condemnation for the religious leadership that claimed special status with God, yet while doing so violated the very heart of what God's kingdom represents. The last thing Jesus will tolerate is their using this woman to serve their selfish, misguided, and evil attempts to oppose what he considers to be the will of God.

How do you think Jesus is feeling during this incident? Given his attitude toward the Pharisees, distrusting their motives (as well he should!), despising their eagerness to *use* this woman and humiliate her in public just to get at him (and in the process reduce her, a child of God, to an object, a thing, rather than a person), how do you think he feels? This is how I see it . . . Watch him seething inside. Observe the level of anger rising, coming gradually to the surface. Sometimes anger is not expressed with an increased volume of the voice. Sometimes a person can get angry without throwing things or turning red in the face. Sometimes, I suppose, some people express anger by writing in the dirt.

How could Jesus not be angry in the face of such blatant hypocrisy and godlessness? Channeling his anger into a response that leaves them utterly defenseless, he says, *Let anyone who is without sin be the first one to throw a stone at her.*

There is ample evidence that the Pharisees are not at all interested in the issue of adultery, nor is their main purpose to defend the Law—the Law that has definite, prescribed responses to such behavior. They are solely using the woman to get Jesus. If they are concerned so much with preserving morality and fulfilling the Law, why do they not bring to the temple with the woman the man who is involved in the adultery with her? After all, the Law is very clear: "If a man is caught lying with the wife of another man, both of them shall die" (Deuteronomy 22:22).

This could simply be passed off as a double standard in

a time and culture dominated by men. When I served on the staff of a previous church, I led a series of new member classes. One of the sessions was devoted to a short history of the church. In researching the church's past, I discovered in some old business meeting minutes that a number of years before a woman had been "disfellowshipped" by the congregation. Why? She was seen leaving town in the company of a "certain gentleman." I couldn't help but wonder why the woman's church membership was withdrawn while the man remained a "gentleman"! But this situation in the temple isn't merely a case of a double standard. The Pharisees don't care one whit if the Law is fulfilled. They just want to discredit Jesus.

But the woman doesn't know that. As far as she is concerned, this could very well be a life-or-death situation for her. How is she to know she is merely a pawn in the Pharisees's chess game? As far as she is aware of it, they have every intention of carrying out the sentence of the Law. "If a man is caught lying with the wife of another man, both of them shall die..."

She doesn't know Jesus from Adam. All he has to do is say the word and she's a goner! "You're right, boys. That's what the Law says. Do what you have to do." All this, not to mention the public shame of being hauled in front of everyone in the temple and labeled a sinner deserving death. They might as well have hung an "A" around her neck and then burned her at the stake.

"Well, what do you have to say about this woman?" Saying not a word, Jesus bends over and starts writing with his finger on the ground. Our tendency is to wonder why he does that, or to conjecture as to what he might be writing. But I want you to look into the terror-stricken face of the woman. What do you suppose is going on in her mind and heart as Jesus stoops over to write on the ground? Remember, she doesn't know the conflict that is going on between Jesus and the Pharisees. She only knows what she can see, and what she sees most clearly is that she is in a lot of trouble.

Is Jesus making out a list of those who will be included in the execution party? Is he writing down the Levitical law that condemns her to die? Is he stalling in order to accentuate her public shame? From her perspective it appears the only thing he is doing is putting off the inevitable. Can you imagine the agony she is feeling while he casually plays in the dirt?!

But then, watch her carefully when she hears Jesus slowly and clearly utter the magical words, *Let anyone who is without sin be the first one to throw a stone at her.* She is as astonished as anyone else by the simple but profound response of the young rabbi.

One by one the Pharisees walk away. It isn't as if the force of what he says hits them like a lightning bolt, to the point that they are running over one another to get out of there, to escape. No, the impact of his biting and righteous words have a slow and gradual effect upon them. The realization of what he says begins slowly to seep in, gradually, gradually, until each of them—beginning with the elders, John says—begin drifting away, no doubt absorbing the volatility and the *rightness* of his words. *Let anyone who is without sin be the first one to throw a stone at her.* There is no one—no, not one—who is without sin. The stones would lie silent that day.

Jesus's writing on the ground the first time is his way of letting the Pharisees know he is not going to play their game.

When he does it again, he is telling them clearly that he is through with them. They can go now; the game is over. He has no desire to talk with them any further.

After they are all gone, Jesus speaks finally to the woman. Thus far she is merely a pawn in the hands of the Pharisees, thus has no voice in the matter. *Woman*—it is the same word, incidentally, that he uses to address his mother—*Woman, where have they gone*? It is a rhetorical question, of course. He knows where they've gone; back to their little vipers's nests, nursing their wounds. *Does no one condemn you*? Of course no one condemns her. Jesus has framed the question in such a way that no one in his right mind would have pressed the issue.

Then comes the pivotal response. *Neither do I condemn you.* He is the only one who has the right to condemn her. He is the only one in this situation who knows no sin. But neither does he choose to condemn her. Jesus is on the side of God, and God is not in the business of condemning. *Redemption* is operative in the kingdom, not condemnation. *Neither do I condemn you. Go your way, and from now on do not sin again.*

Let's consider again how the woman is feeling about all this. Is it possible—could it be—that this rabbi with the Galilean accent is not like the rest of the condemning religious leaders? Are her ears deceiving her? Did he actually say he would not condemn her? Was she really and truly going to get off that easily?

Yes and no. Jesus would not condemn her, that is true. But neither would he let her off easily. *Go your way*, he says to her, *and from now on **do not sin again***. That is *not* getting off easily. Jesus is not letting her off the hook. Redemption is not the easy way out.

Do not sin again, he says. It is Jesus's way of telling her that she has been offered a new life. Forgiveness is hers. It is not dependent on her right behavior in the future. It is completely unmerited. Even though she didn't ask for it, any more than did the paralytic in Capernaum who was let down through the roof of the house by his friends, she is forgiven. Her past is wiped clean. Now she needs to take advantage of it. She is not to return to her bed of adultery. She is to accept God's eternal gift, and to do it now. She is to turn her back on what she has been and turn her future to what she can be. It would not be easy.

Unfortunately, Jesus's admonition to the woman has found itself in the hands of those who do not know its context, and frankly, don't care. Like the Pharisees who used the woman for their own purposes, a number of people have taken what Jesus said and used it to get themselves off the hook, to relieve themselves easily of whatever situation they found themselves in. That is unfortunate. This story does not mean that Jesus is loose when it comes to inappropriate sexual behavior. It is included to show that the Pharisees's blind and self-serving adherence to legalism was just as wrong and sinful as the behavior of the woman.

The Pharisees leave the temple, presumably to go sulk over losing this latest skirmish with Jesus. They will eventually garner up enough nerve to go after him again, and Jesus knows it. In other words, they will learn no redemptive lesson from this painful encounter with the Nazarene. But the adulterous woman has the possibility of taking on a whole new, transforming way of life.

She is not easily excused from her past behavior. She is forgiven it; make no mistake about that. But then, she is admonished to return to it no longer. The Pharisees learn nothing; the woman discovers everything. The Pharisees have been given just as much opportunity for redemption as the woman, or anybody else Jesus encountered. They choose not to accept it.

We assume the woman did accept Jesus's generous gift of redemption, but there is no evidence to bear that out. The issue of forgiveness is not questioned. She is forgiven. Jesus makes that clear. *Neither do I condemn you*, he says to her. Whether she accepted it, we do not know.

This is what we do know . . . When we stand before Christ with our behavior laid open before him, he essentially says the same to us as he did to this nameless woman. *Neither do I condemn you.* Our sin is forgiven. But scripture, as well as Jesus's gracious forgiveness, is always open-ended and always calls for a response. Whether John framed the ending of his story as he did for that purpose we cannot know. But as we watch the shadows of the temple engulf this woman as she departs, we are left with this eerie feeling that it is not just she who is leaving, having had her sinful life forgiven. We too walk in her steps with Jesus's words echoing in our minds and hearts. *Neither do I condemn you. Neither do I condemn you. Neither do I condemn you.* But then, to add balance to that unmerited forgiveness, we also hear him say, *Go your way, and from now on do not sin again.*

What does that mean? Perhaps it is this . . . Don't go back to your old way of life. Accept the unmerited forgiveness

Jesus offers you, but understand that with such forgiveness comes the relationship with him that is a daily journey of faith. Such a journey takes us forward, not backwards. It leads us to glimpses of the kingdom we have never seen before, and offers us opportunities of grace we don't deserve.

So when you hear Jesus say to you, *Neither do I condemn you*, accept his unmerited forgiveness and never look back. I'd like to think that is what this woman did, wouldn't you? Why don't we do the same?

MARY MAGDALENE

"I Have Seen The Lord"

Do not hold on to me, because I have not yet ascended to the Father. But go to my brothers and say to them, "I am ascending to my Father and your Father, to my God and your God" (John 20:17).

Life teaches us a number of lessons, lessons that tend to stay with us through the ages. For example, a friend shared with me a number of years ago that there are four basic emotions in life: *mad*, *sad*, *glad*, and *scared*. I will never forget that, and often find this knowledge to be of help when I am going through one or all of these emotions. It puts me in touch with myself and helps me determine more effectively what my response to certain situations ought to be.

Another lesson I learned fairly early as a pastor is that a reputation—whether it be the reputation of an individual, a family, or even a church—is an easy thing to get but is very difficult to lose. That is the case with the woman we meet in the gospels named Mary, who was from the village of Magdala. Some of the things that we think we know about her may not be true at all, and are actually a part of later Christian tradition, tradition that is based on erroneous information or assumptions. She has a reputation that is largely not accurate and is not deserved. And let us not forget, a reputation is an easy thing to get, but it is very difficult to lose.

Mary Magdalene has the reputation of having been a "sinful woman," a euphemism for her being a prostitute. In the seventh chapter of Luke's gospel, the story is told of Jesus' visit to the home of a Pharisee. While they were eating, a woman of the city, "who was a sinner," Luke says, brought an alabaster jar of ointment to the gathering. It was not unusual, given the culture of that day, for outsiders to crash such social occasions. She stood behind Jesus weeping, and began to bathe his feet with her tears and dry them with her hair. Then she anointed his feet with the ointment. *Therefore, I tell you,* Jesus says to his host, *her sins, which were many, have been forgiven; hence she has shown great love* (v. 47).

During the Patristic and Medieval periods, the woman in Luke's story somehow came to be associated with Mary Magdalene. As the tradition developed, since this woman once possessed many sins, it follows that she must have been a prostitute. She is portrayed that way in the movie, *The Last Temptation of Christ*, in the musical *Jesus Christ, Superstar,* and in Mel Gibson's *The Passion of the Christ.* Oh, that Hollywood would get it right and do better hermeneutical research! But this line of reasoning has also found its way into many writings and sermons. Yet, there is absolutely no biblical evidence to bear this out. A reputation is an easy thing to get, but it is very difficult to lose. Just ask Mary of Magdala.

Let's attempt to set the record straight, and consider Mary in light of what we do know. What we do know is that she had once been possessed by seven demons. The story of how she was freed from her torment is not detailed. Luke tells us of this after the fact. By the time we meet Mary, she has already become a follower of Jesus. Evidently, she and some other women provided for Jesus and his disciples out of their own financial resources, and they served him with their presence and devotion.

Seven demons. In anybody's book, that's a tough row to hoe. Belief in demon possession was rampant in the first century and covered a lot of possibilities. Think of the others in the New Testament who were depicted as being demon-possessed. There is the Gadarene demoniac, who has so many demons his name is "Legion." There is the boy who reveals all the classic signs of epilepsy. When Jesus comes down from the Mount of Transfiguration, he finds that his disciples have been unable to effect any kind of cure for him. In both of these stories, the gospel writers go into quite a bit of detail to let us know what is wrong with those who are possessed. Yet, that is not true of Mary Magdalene. The fact that she had once been possessed by seven demons is merely mentioned by Luke, but he does not tell us how those demons were removed.

It's almost as if the gospel writers don't want to talk very much about Mary. Yet, she is the only woman mentioned in all four gospels as having been present at both the crucifixion and the tomb. It would seem that her level of devotion to her Lord is unmatched by anyone, including the disciples! Yet, this story in John's gospel is the only one that portrays very much about her. Strange, isn't it? Why do you think that is so?

Is it because she is a woman? Possibly. It was a man's

world, you know. Did the gospel writers not find her healing story to be compelling enough to include it in their accounts of Jesus' life and ministry? Wouldn't you think seven demons would be compelling enough? Were they jealous of her devotion to Jesus and of his allegiance to her?

It is hard to imagine what demon possession might have been like, any more than it would be reasonable for a perfectly sane person to describe how it feels to be mentally ill. But if Mary Magdalene had seven demons, it is probably accurate to say that she—and this would be an understatement—was in really bad shape. It should also be safe to assume that after being healed, her gratitude and devotion to Jesus would have been equal to the level of her healing. Much healing was required and much devotion followed. And one thing we do know about Mary, despite the scant evidence in scripture, is that her dedication to her Lord was quite remarkable.

Yet, admit it now: if there is one woman you would choose as a model of faith, one you would want to emulate in your own walk with Christ, one you would look up to more than any other, of those we have considered in this book, or any other you know about in scripture, it would probably not be Mary Magdalene, would it? Why do you think that is? The chances are, it is because we don't know much about her. And . . . she had once been demon-possessed. In addition, we tend to think, even though there is no scriptural evidence for it, that she had once been a prostitute.

Frankly, it is hard for us to allow her to be forgiven all that, isn't it? Yet, after all is said and done, the scriptural record, as thin as it may be, does reveal that she was wholly dedicated to her Master, and there was obviously a great deal of affection between her and Jesus. After all, by John's account, he appeared to her first after the resurrection. Not to the remaining eleven disciples, but to Mary.

With that as background, let's look more closely at the story, shall we?

Anyone who has attended an Easter sunrise service knows what it is like to get up before the crack of dawn, make his or her way down to the location of the service, stumble around in the wet dew, figure out a seating place, and try to be ready for the first ray of sunlight. Imagine what it might have been like for Mary that first Easter morning as she makes her way to the place where they have laid her Master and Lord. The darkness, the unfamiliarity with the gravesite, the grief.

That is one thing we don't often bring to our sunrise services: grief. Instead, we come with expectation and great joy. Mary had no reason to have such feelings. She only knew grief, confusion, and fear. And her sole interest on that first Easter morning is the proper care of a corpse. Little did she know there would be none.

Note the detail in John's story. The other disciple outruns Simon Peter (because he is younger?) but stops at the door. When Simon Peter arrives after him, true to his impetuous nature, he barges right in. This seems to give courage to the other disciple, and he follows. They discover the linen cloths which had been wrapped around Jesus' body. Again, note the detail. John tells us the head cloth was not lying with the other wrappings but was in a place by itself. After seeing this, they go back home.

What do you mean they go home? That's all? And John

says the other disciple believed. Believed what? That Jesus's body was no longer there? That was obvious. You didn't have to be Sherlock Holmes to figure that out. What is it the other disciple believed?

John admits they didn't understand that Jesus would have risen from the dead. So they just . . . went . . . home. To wait until sunlight perhaps? Or to discuss it with the other disciples, to see if they could figure out any of this? Or, to think about what all this means? Or . . . well, truth be told, we don't know what they intended to do. We just know they went home.

But not Mary. She stayed, stayed and wept. We can probably make a fair guess that a few desperate prayers were mumbled in the midst of her sobs. Did Mary not have a home to go to? The scriptures make no mention of Mary having a family. She is from Galilee, as was Jesus. Perhaps Jesus represented home to Mary.

There is comfort in being home. After a particularly difficult time in a previous church, and then two years spent healing from it, our family came back home to our native state. In a real sense, we found acceptance here as perhaps in no other place we have lived. We understood the culture, and the native folk understood us. There is comfort in being home.

Does Mary have a home to go to? If indeed Jesus represented home to Mary, now that he is in a tomb, there is a sense in which, in her grief and despair, the tomb has now become Mary's home.

In Edinburgh, Scotland there is a monument to a Scottish Terrier named Greyfriar's Bobby. As the story is told, his master died, and for fourteen years, day after day, the terrier would make his way to the cemetery in the center of the city where he would spend the day lying on his master's grave. The residents were so touched by his loyalty that his story was published and a monument erected. His master's grave became his home.

Has the sepulcher become Mary's home? If so, what does she do now, for the tomb is empty?

Jesus was her center, her life. Ever since that fateful day when he freed her from the terrible torment of demon possession, she had loved Jesus, followed Jesus, served Jesus.

Now, not only is Jesus dead, she doesn't even know what happened to his body. Mary is spinning in her grief, tormented in a way that not even seven demons can equal.

Mary's weeping, perhaps, is a combination of grief, confusion, and fear. Grief because the Master and Teacher to whom she was so devoted has died a merciless and painful death. Confusion over why the tomb is empty. Fear over what could possibly be the gruesome motive behind someone's stealing Jesus's body.

But there's a bit of curiosity in the mix as well. As she weeps, she bends over to peer into the tomb. She knows the door was removed. She knows that Jesus's body is no longer in the tomb. She is aware of that because Simon Peter and the other disciples have confirmed it. She doesn't have to go in to know the tomb is empty. But she can't help herself. No doubt, her grief and confusion and fear are mixed with curiosity. She wants to see the empty tomb for herself.

"Woman, why are you weeping?" Angels? She sees angels, one where Jesus's head had been, the other sitting where his feet had been. Angels . . . of all things, angels!

Normally, when angels are included in any of the gospel narratives, they have quite a big job to do. Their participation is extensive, and their message involved. If you are an angel sent on a holy mission—and what other kind of mission would be entrusted to an angel?—you expect no less. So, it makes you wonder why there are angels in John's account of the resurrection. Were they really necessary? All they do is ask Mary why she is weeping. Evidently, that is the only job given them. Why bother? In just a moment, Jesus is going to ask her the very same thing. Isn't it a bit redundant? Why the angels? Why send angels to do what Jesus will be doing himself?

Maybe they are there to provide the clue that the tomb is empty because of divine activity and intervention. Their presence is more important than their words. Yet, they only get to ask one measly, little question. "Woman, why are you weeping?" They don't even get to tell Mary why Jesus's body is not there.

Still, even with their presence, when Mary leaves the empty tomb she is as confused as she was when she first got there.

"Woman, why are you weeping?"

"Leave the weeping for those who have real reason to grieve. This may be a tomb, but there is no death here. There is no weeping where there is no confusion. Mary, you shouldn't be confused. The tomb is empty because it isn't powerful enough to contain our Lord. You should have no fear, no confusion. You should have no grief. No one has taken Jesus's body."

Easy enough for them to say. Do you still doubt that

Mary is confused? When she turns and sees Jesus, she thinks he's the gardener. That's confused!

Woman, why are you weeping? There's that question again. *Whom are you looking for*?

Not only does Mary think Jesus is the gardener, somehow she thinks he is responsible for the empty tomb. He is, of course, but not in the way she thinks. Still think she's not confused? "Sir, if you have carried him away, tell me where you laid him, and I will take him away."

Obviously, Mary's grief and fear and confusion have clouded her thinking abilities. If someone had stolen or taken Jesus's body, doesn't it make sense that they would have removed his body with the burial cloths intact? Why take the time and the pains to unwrap them? Wouldn't grave robbers be in a hurry? Or did Mary think the gardener would not want a criminal in one of *his* graves, so he had the body removed? It is strange logic, isn't it?

Or, there isn't any logic to it at all. Logic is in short supply when grief and fear and confusion are found in abundance. "Sir, tell me where you have laid him."

John removes our suspense by informing us of Jesus' identity, something Mary doesn't know at this point in the story. We know she isn't talking to the gardener but to the risen Lord. We know what she doesn't know. Jesus, unknown to Mary, asks her, *Whom are you looking for*? Why does he ask her this? What does he mean by it? He knows whom she's looking for. Why doesn't he identify himself to her immediately? Is he getting some kind of perverted joy out of stringing her along? *Whom are you looking for*?

She's looking for a corpse. That's what she's looking

for—a corpse. Sometimes, when our expectations are the lowest, God, in his mercy and love, reaches down and graces us with his highest. That is what God does for Mary. We don't know if it is her reward for being so devoted to her Lord. We only know she is the first to see the risen Christ. Of all the people Jesus called to follow him, Mary of Magdala, once possessed by seven demons, is the first to see Christ, her risen Lord.

Mary. We all like to hear someone call our name, don't we? *Mary.* Can you imagine how she must have felt? From the deepest grief to the highest joy, just in the hearing of her name. What an emotional roller coaster! Just by the hearing of her name.

But it isn't just the hearing of her name. It is the familiar voice. The joy is found in knowing the *One* who says it.

Or maybe it is the way he says it. *Mary.* Are you familiar with Luke's story of the dejected followers walking from Jerusalem to their home in Emmaus? When they left Jerusalem, Jesus was dead. The only thing they can think of, as they trek back home, is that terrible image of his cross silhouetted against the dark, angry sky. A stranger joins them on their way. They tell him the story of how their Master, Jesus of Nazareth, has been crucified.

When they reach their destination, they invite the stranger to join them for a meal. He does so, and it is when he breaks bread with them that they realize he is no stranger at all. He is Jesus, their risen Lord! He is identified to them just by the familiar way he breaks the bread.

And Mary knows him, just by the way he calls her name. *Mary.* Perhaps it is the way he says it. Or she recognizes his voice—the voice that demanded the demons leave her, the voice that wove for the disciples stories of the kingdom of heaven, the voice that commanded the storms to cease and the cripples to walk and the dead to rise again. *That* voice.

We really don't know, do we? But it may very well have been that Jesus did not want Mary to know who he was until that very moment he called her name.

How long has it been since Jesus called your name? He does, you know. Perhaps a better question is, how long since you heard him call your name? He calls to you, and to me, to make his presence known to us. The only question remaining is, do we hear him? And if we do, how do we respond? If we are like Mary, it could very well be that the level of our dedication to Jesus is in direct proportion to how forgiven we feel.

To those who have accepted the forgiveness of the risen Christ, every day is Easter. The risen Christ comes to us, calling our name. How we respond to his voice has eternal consequences. So when you hear him call your name, give him an attentive ear. Even if your name isn't Mary, you too can say, "I have seen the Lord!"

FEMININE FACES:

PROFILES OF BIBLICAL WOMEN OF FAITH

STUDY GUIDE

A PERSONAL WORD FROM THE AUTHOR

While I would not describe my approach to the study and interpretation of scripture as being solely confessional, neither do I do so with the idea in mind that I have all the answers. In fact, this exploration of women in the Bible may ask more questions than it provides answers. For that reason, this study guide is included as a means for the reader to dialogue with what has preceded it in these pages.

This guide can be used on both the individual and group level. However, I do believe it will be most effective when used in a small-group setting, such as a Sunday School class or cell group. As a minister, with the inevitable sermon awaiting me each week, I often find that discussing the kernel of an idea with someone else gets my creative juices flowing. Expressing my thoughts to a friend or acquaintance, in a free-form, conversational way, enables me to get in touch with thoughts that up to that point have been suppressed in my subconscious. How many times I have wished for a tape recorder, in order to record my own words and thoughts as I convey them to another person! I envision the same dynamic for processing one's reactions to the ideas expressed in this book.

However you choose to use this guide, please do so with one purpose in mind: to enlarge your understanding, as well as appreciation, for these tremendous women of faith who have taught us valuable lessons on how to live out our own. I do believe the effort will be well worth it, and you will find yourself being encouraged by the lessons they continue to teach us.

God Bless,
Randy Hyde

EVE

"The Mother of Us All"

For background, read *Genesis 2:18-3:24*.

Reflect on the following statement by the author: "Eve's demise began when she first started giving credence to the serpent's enticing message." Do you agree? If so, why? Do you disagree? If so, why?

When it comes to your own temptations, does Eve's experience reflect your own?

The question is asked, "Have you ever wondered why the serpent approached the woman?" (as opposed to the man). The author offers some possibilities. Do you have your own ideas? What are they?

According to the author of this story in Genesis, God told the man and woman that if they ate from the forbidden tree they would die. The serpent negates this notion, and it appears the serpent is right. How would you explain this seeming discrepancy?

Do you think the first woman is to blame for the "first" sin?

Are you familiar with the expression, often used in the context of a wedding ceremony, of a man and a woman becoming "one flesh"? What does that mean in the context of this story?

The author states that after God confronts the first couple, they must now "operate out of their own resources." What does that mean to you?

When God confronts Adam and Eve about their sin, the man responds even though, according to the story, the serpent has tempted the woman. Why do you think that is?

From your own faith and life experience, answer the question asked by the author: "Can God be trusted?"

SARAH

"MOTHER OF LAUGHTER"

For background, read *Genesis 12-25:10*.

Was God fair to Sarah (and to Abraham), or do you feel that God used Sarah to do what God wanted?

Discuss, or think about, the issue of fairness and grace. Are they synonymous? If not, what is the difference? How would you prefer that God relate to you?

Why do you think, according to this story in Genesis, that God spoke only to Abraham and never to Sarah?

When the messengers of God informed Abraham that he and Sarah would have a son, we are told that Sarah laughed. What do you think was the source of her laughter?

Today, how do you think God intervenes in seemingly hopeless situations, such as Sarah's?

Is anything too wonderful for the Lord? is what the messengers of God say to Abraham . . . and thus to Sarah. What does that mean to you? Do you believe it?

Reflect on this final statement in the chapter on Sarah: "[W]e journey together toward the kingdom of God. And we do it amidst fear and faith, with tears and great laughter. And maybe, just maybe, it is the laughter that God blesses the most." Think about the times and ways God has come to you in the midst of both laughter and pain. If in a group, discuss it.

REBEKAH

"AT ANY COST"

For background, read *Genesis 25:19-27:46.*

The theme of barrenness continues in Rebekah's story, and will be seen again in Hannah's. Why do you think this is so important to the story of the Israelites?

Unlike Sarah, God speaks directly to Rebekah. The author suggests a couple of possibilities for why that is true. What do you think?

Reflect on the Old Testament concept of the *blessing*. Is a blessing secured by deceit still a blessing?

Why do you suppose God used such a dysfunctional family to do God's will?

Does this story prove to be the exception to the rule; namely, that the ends are not justified by the means?

Rebekah seems to go to great extremes to fulfill God's wishes. To what extent will we seek to do God's will?

MIRIAM

"The Singer"

For background, read *Exodus 2:1-10, 15:1-21* and *Numbers 12.*

The author makes the point that major events in life begin with the smallest of deeds. Do you believe that? If so, can you think of small events in your life that have led to big consequences?

Though Moses is obviously portrayed more prominently in the telling of the Hebrew story, leadership characteristics found in his life are equally visible in his sister Miriam. What are they? Identify the characteristics you may have inherited. What are they? How have they contributed to your life?

The author encourages reading between the lines of this biblical story in order to observe it, as much as possible, from Miriam's point of view. What would you add to the story from your perspective?

What does this story teach us about the difference between fate and

God's purposeful will?

Ironically, God is not mentioned in the story of Miriam's effort to save her baby brother Moses. Yet, when it comes time to celebrate the freedom of the Israelites, Miriam gives credit to Yahweh. Why?

What to you are the mustard seeds of life?

RUTH

"WHITHERSOEVER"

For background, read the entire book of *Ruth*.

Naomi says to Ruth, "[T]he hand of the Lord has turned against me." This implies a theology of "cause and effect," that if bad things happen to people, whether they are good or bad, it is the Lord's doing. Do you believe that? If not, how do you explain such things?

The author suggests, because of difficult circumstances, that Naomi has "shuttered up her life." Has that ever happened to you? Did you overcome it? If so, how? If not, what is keeping you from doing so?

Have you ever, when confronted by a difficult circumstance, been tempted to do as Naomi said to Ruth, "Turn back"? If so, did you do it? What have been the consequences of your decision? If you did not turn back, can you relate what the results were of that decision?

Ellen van Wolde says that Ruth "gives up everything without knowing what she will get back in return." In fact, it appears that Naomi doesn't appreciate the kind gesture. Why do you think Ruth would be so faithful to a mother-in-law who is so bitter?

Reflect on the level of risk in your life, especially when it comes to your faith journey. What does Ruth's story teach you about expanding your risk level?

HANNAH

"The Meaning of Sacrifice"

For background, read *1 Samuel 1:1-4:1*.

Have you ever bargained with God? What were the circumstances? What was the result?

The subject of barrenness is once again seen in Hannah's situation. Why do you think it is such a prevalent theme in the Old Testament?

How does Hannah's story illustrate God's patience with Israel?

Bitterness over her situation seems to drive Hannah to God. Has that ever been true in your life?

The Old Testament appears to support the idea that barrenness was proof of God's disfavor. How do you reconcile this personally?

What can you learn from this story, despite discomfort with some of the interpretative elements of it; namely, that God caused Hannah's barrenness?

Hannah prays to the "Lord of hosts," a militaristic term for God. What does that tell you about the way she views her situation?

Hannah is not entirely blameless. In her desperate bargain with God, she makes promises for her yet unborn child that will affect him for all his life. How do you feel about that?

What does the word "sacrifice" mean to you? The author suggests that it be defined in a new light as *consecration*. Do you agree?

Is the idea of sacrifice threatening to you?

Are you willing to trust God with the "what ifs" of your life?

MARY, THE MOTHER OF JESUS

"more than a mother can take"

For background, read *Luke 1:1-2:52*, *John 2:1-11*, *Mark 3:31-35* (and parallel passages).

Do you believe in angels? Do you believe they exist now or only visited humans during biblical times? Is it necessary for you to believe in angels to be a person of faith?

Even if you do not believe in the existence of angels, imagine what such a visit might be like, as took place between Mary and the messenger of God. Put yourself in Mary's place and consider the conversation, not to mention emotions, that such an encounter might engender. Make this imagining a devotional exercise.

Did Mary, in saying, "Here am I, the servant of the Lord; let it be to me according to your word," speak too soon? Would you have responded so quickly?

Why do you think Mary represents a scriptural about-face in regard to the theme of barrenness?

The only way to see an issue clearly is to live it, then look back upon it and analyze it. Again, put yourself in Mary's place. She is near the end of her life and she ponders all these things in her heart. In regard to the issue of bringing God's own unique Son into the world, what do you think might come first to her mind? Make this a devotional exercise.

Do you think it was necessary for Mary to discipline her young son? If so, how do you think she did it?

At the wedding in Cana, was Mary telling Jesus it was time for him to "show his stuff?" How do you interpret Jesus' response? Was he showing disrespect to Mary by answering her as he did?

Though Jesus's response in Capernaum surely weighed heavily on Mary's heart, it does define more clearly how we can have relationship with him. How so?

To what extent can you echo Mary's commitment, "Let it be to me according to your word"?

MARY OF BETHANY

"THE BETTER PART"

For background, read *Luke 10:38-42* and *John 11:1-46.*

In the regard to the discussion of Mary and her sister Martha, the author discusses sibling relationships. Consider your own and reflect upon what might have led to this exchange between Jesus and Martha.

What is the better part that Mary has chosen and Martha has not? Do you agree with the author's interpretation? If not, what is your explanation?

Do you find yourself relating more to Martha than to Mary? If so, why?

How does Jesus elevate and/or change the role of women in his day? Did he go far enough? In keeping with his spirit and purpose, what can you do to encourage the women you know to follow Mary's example?

How does Jesus's spirit of liberation toward Mary (and all women) affect us all?

How does this unique story reflect your current personal value to the kingdom of heaven?

MARTHA

"True Believer"

For background, read *Luke 10:38-42* and *John 11:1-46* (the same as for the previous chapter).

The author mentions grief that has "frustration and perplexity and questioning added to the mix." Have you ever experienced grief like that? If so, how did you cope? How do you find yourself coping now?

While Martha changes focus—from food preparation to rushing to see Jesus—she still stays true to form, to her personality, by engaging him in a direct and rather confrontational conversation. Does this confirm or change your opinion of Martha?

In regard to the issue of emotional bank accounts, have you ever made a withdrawal in a relationship with someone significant to you? Has a friend or loved one done the same to you? How have you reacted? Is the relationship still intact? If so, how? If not, why?

What is your first reaction to Martha? Do you see her as a person of strong faith? If not, why? If so, what is it that makes you think of her as a faithful follower and friend of Jesus?

Why do you think it was so important to Jesus that Martha believe in him and the power of resurrection through him?

Do you think that Martha's confession of faith is every bit as important as Peter's "Great Confession?"

Do you think it is significant that Jesus demands—and Martha voices—this level of faith before Lazarus is resurrected?

Do you have any relationships based on what you can do for the other person? On what the other person can do for you? Consider this in light of the friendship between Jesus and Martha.

THE WOMAN AT THE WELL

"LIVING WATER"

For background, read *John 4:1-42.*

Can you count the number of social/religious customs Jesus broke in his encounter with the woman at the well at Sychar?

How important are customs and social rules (even unwritten ones) to you?

How long does it take, when you meet a person, to see in him or her that which is less than obvious?

In this encounter with the Samaritan woman, Jesus describes himself and his mission in terms of water, living water. What other imageries can you think of that apply to Jesus?

What does forgiveness mean to you? What comes to your mind first, and most importantly, when you think of how you have found forgiveness?

The author suggests that following Jesus is to leave your "jar" behind. What are you willing to leave in the jar when you do so?

THE WOMAN TAKEN IN ADULTERY

"unmerited forgiveness"

For background, read *Leviticus 20:10-16* and *John 8:1-11.*

Has the author appropriately described the backdrop to this encounter between Jesus and the religious establishment? Is it important in order to understand the dynamics behind this story?

In reading this chapter, did you answer the questions put forth by the author?

"How did they (the Pharisees) find her? Did they know of her "lifestyle" before this incident with Jesus? Had they ignored it up to now, deciding to do something about it only when it would suit their purposes?"

Why do you think Jesus took the time to write on the ground?

Let anyone who is without sin be the first one to throw a stone at her. The author describes this statement with the words *volatility* and *rightness*. What words would you use to describe his response to the Pharisees?

Jesus's response puts the Pharisees in an unwinnable situation. Has he ever put you in a place where you only had one possible response?

Did Jesus let the woman off easily?

Why is the context for this story so important?

In this encounter, did Jesus offer redemption to the Pharisees as well as to the adulterous woman?

Is there such a thing as forgiveness/redemption without relationship?

MARY MAGDALENE

"I Have Seen the Lord"

For background, read *Luke 8:1-3*, *Mark 15:40-16:8*, and *John 19:25-20:18*.

Why is it important to try to understand the Mary of Magdala portrayed in scripture and not the one known through tradition?

Why do you think Mary Magdalene is not given more respect in the biblical/Christian community of faith?

Why do you think Jesus appeared first to Mary after the resurrection? Was it because of his initiative or hers?

Do you agree with the author that perhaps Jesus represented *home* to Mary?

What happens to grief when confusion is added to the mix?

Why did Mary not think logically at the grave?

Has God ever called you by name? If so, how? When? Where? How did you respond?

COVER ART KEY

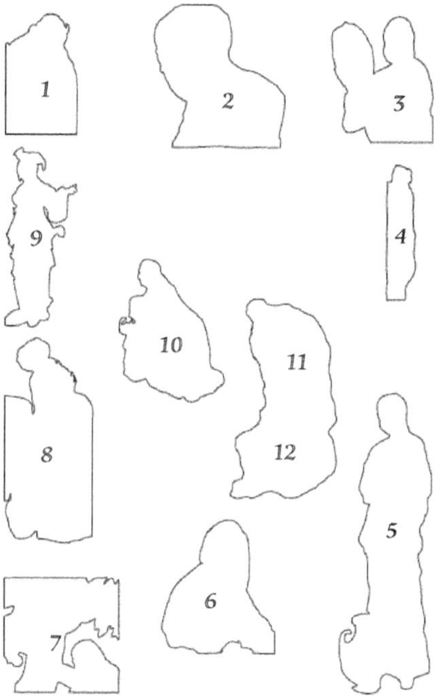

1. Caravaggio, *The Repentant Magdalene*; 2. Cranach (The Elder), *The Woman Taken in Adultery*; 3. Feuerbach, *Miriam*; 4. Provost, *Sarah*; 5. Poussin, *Rebekah*; 6. Bellini, *Mary, Mother of Jesus*; 7. Titian, *Eve and the Serpent*; 8. de Flandes, *The Woman at the Well*; 9. van Score, *Ruth*; van den Eeckhout, *Hannah Presenting Samuel at the Temple*; 11. Tintoretto, *Martha*; 12. Tintoretto, *Mary of Bethany*

www.ingramcontent.com/pod-product-compliance
Lightning Source LLC
Chambersburg PA
CBHW032100080426
42733CB00006B/351
* 9 7 8 0 9 8 2 9 4 1 3 6 2 *